WILLIAMS-SONOMA

Grilling & Roasting

The Best of Williams-Sonoma Lifestyles Series

Grilling & Roasting

GENERAL EDITOR
CHUCK WILLIAMS

RECIPE PHOTOGRAPHY
RICHARD ESKITE

Oxmoor House®

Contents

Introduction

Grilling and roasting are two ancient cooking techniques that have much in common: both subject food to dry, often intense heat in order to achieve dishes that are richly browned and flavorful outside, moist and tender within. Whether you are grilling or roasting, the recipes in this book stress the importance of seasoning your meat, poultry, fish, and vegetables well prior to cooking. This helps contribute to the flavor and keeps the food juicy and tender.

For most people, there is a grilling "season," the window of time between the spring and the fall when it is warm enough to grill outdoors. However, during the winter months, you can achieve the same wonderful and deliciously caramelized taste, by roasting—or even broiling—your favorite foods in the oven.

MODERN GRILLING

Grilling has come a long way from the days when the outdoor menu was limited to steaks, chicken, and burgers. Those old favorites are still delicious, of course, but cooks today feel free to toss a wide array of items—meat, poultry, fish, seafood, vegetables, even breads—onto the grill. In addition, grilling enthusiasts readily draw on grilling traditions that span the world, supplementing the more traditional Red-Hot Barbecue Chicken (page 59) and Grilled Peppery Rib-Eye Steak with Roquefort Butter (page 121) with everything from Tandoori Chicken Wings with Raita (page 29), Shredded Beef with Avocado-Tomatillo Salsa (page 115), and Coconut Shrimp with Lime (page 220).

TYPES OF GRILLS

Charcoal or gas grill? The choice is yours. While you cannot beat the unique flavor of charcoal-cooked food, a charcoal grill cannot match the simple operation and clean-up of a gas grill. Some feel the charcoal itself is too bulky and the ashes are a headache to dispose of. That may be true, but the inarguable virtue of a charcoal grill is the heat, which creates the smoky flavor it produces—the hallmark of perfectly grilled food. On the other hand, the easy operation of gas grills has made them extremely popular, as the propane flame evenly distributes heat throughout the cooking area. While food cooked on the gas grill lacks distinctive charcoal flavor, it is hard to beat the grill's convenience.

Regardless of the grill you use, it is important to learn first how to set up a grill for cooking using either direct or indirect heat, depending on the food, and to test the foods cooked on it for doneness.

SETTING UP A GRILL FOR COOKING

The first thing to do when you're ready to cook is to ignite the charcoal or preheat a gas grill. Many cooks today feel that lighter fluid imparts an unpleasant flavor to food when it is used to ignite charcoal briquettes. An alternative is to use a chimney starter, whose ingenious design allows you to start a fire without chemicals. To use a chimney starter, insert a few sheets of crumpled newspaper in the bottom grate, and then mound charcoal in the top of the chimney. Place the chimney on a heatproof surface and ignite the paper. The flames will burn upward, igniting the coals. When the coals are covered with gray ash, in about 25 minutes, tip them carefully onto the fire grate. If you are using a gas grill, preheat it for about 15 minutes with the lid closed.

Next, determine whether you will be grilling with direct-heat cooking (used for relatively thin food such as burgers, steaks, chops, fish fillets, and skewered food) or indirect-heat cooking (used for larger pieces of food such as roasts, whole birds, and ribs). To prepare a charcoal grill for direct-heat cooking, spread the coals in an even layer over the fire bed. For a gas grill, keep on all the burners after preheating. For indirect-heat cooking, arrange the coals in two equal piles on two sides of the grill, leaving the center free of coals. Place an aluminum foil drip pan, half full of water, in

the area between the coals to catch the dripping fat, creating a cool zone for the grill. For a gas grill, turn the middle burner off (on a three-burner grill) or turn off one of the side burners (on a two-burner grill).

Then, evaluate the heat level on a charcoal grill, or adjust the heat on a gas grill, to ensure you will be cooking at the correct temperature. Most of the recipes call for medium-high heat (375°–400°F/ 190°–200°C) or high heat (400°–450°F/200°–230°C). For other heat levels, turn to the chart on page 291. To test the temperature on a charcoal grill, use a grill thermometer or the hand test (see page 291). On a gas grill, simply turn the burner control knobs to the desired heat level.

Last, make sure that the grill grate is clean before you begin cooking. If using a charcoal grill, position the cooking grate over the coals. Use a stiff wire brush to scrub the grill grate well to remove any residual food and grease. For an impeccably clean grill, get in the habit of doing this again after you finish cooking.

CONTROLLING THE HEAT ON THE GRILL

If your food seems to be cooking too fast or flareups occur, try moving the food to a cooler place on the grill rack where the heat is not so intense. You can also cover the grill to douse the flames.

TODAY'S ROASTING

Roasting is a versatile cooking method, perfect for any occasion. It can produce succulent, slow-cooked meals like Provençal Roasted Turkey Breast (page 52) or Pork Loin with Orange-Ginger Glaze (page 166), both of which are suitable for a weekend dinner with family or friends. But roasting is also the perfect choice for quick meals on any day of the week, such as Smoky and Spicy Chicken Breasts (page 56), Mustard Lamb Chops (page 130), or even Roast Fish in Moroccan Marinade (page 208).

EQUIPMENT FOR ROASTING

Roasting needs very little equipment; a roasting pan and oven is all that is required. The best vessels for roasting are heavy-duty aluminum roasting pans with strong, upright handles. Flat or V-shaped roasting racks are also useful when cooking roasts or large birds. When using acidic ingredients, glass or ceramic baking dishes are a better choice than metal roasting pans, as they won't react with the acids. For best results, consider investing in an oven thermometer to check whether your oven is accurate. If it is not, adjust your oven temperature gauge up or down to account for the difference, or have a repair person come to your house to recalibrate your oven.

TYPES OF ROASTING

Roasting no longer relies on the variable heat of an open flame, as it did in ancient times. Instead, today's roasted foods are cooking in a pan in the radiant, dry heat of an enclosed oven set to a specific temperature. The best meats for roasting are tender cuts such as tenderloin, loin, chops, and thick steaks, which are often, although not always, cooked at high temperatures. Poultry, fish, vegetables, and fruits are also good candidates for roasting.

High-temperature roasting—that is, at temperatures of 400°F (200°C) and higher—practically guarantees a tasty, caramelized outer crust and a distinct savory flavor. High temperatures also ensure faster cooking, reducing the time in the kitchen. Most roasting recipes in this book call for moderate temperature roasting, that is, oven settings that range from 300°F (150°C) and up to 400°F (200°C). Foods roasted at moderate temperatures, cook evenly and need less monitoring.

Some recipes use a hybrid roasting technique to gain the desired result. In other words, an initial high temperature is employed to deliver deep surface browning and an intense flavor to the food. Then, the oven is reduced to a moderate or low temperature to help ensure evenly cooked food.

PREPARING FOOD FOR ROASTING

Most of the work associated with roasting is done before the cooking even begins. For example, a roast can be seasoned and refrigerated well before it goes into the oven. Plan ahead, if possible, and allow particularly large cuts of meat, such as whole beef tenderloin, to stand at room temperature for about 1 hour before roasting; let a whole chicken stand for about 30 minutes. Bringing food to room temperature helps to encourage even roasting.

TESTING FOODS FOR DONENESS

Cooking times can vary on the size and shape of the food. When cooking meats or poultry, rely on the internal temperature, not the cooking times, to determine whether or not it is done: Insert an instant-read thermometer into the thickest part of the flesh, away from the bone and note the temperature. If further cooking is required, continue to cook and check again in 5–15 minutes, keeping in mind that temperatures will rise at least 5°F (2°C) while resting. The resting period is an important step in cooking meats or poultry. Don't skimp on it, as the standing time allows the juices to redistribute throughout the flesh. For more information, turn to page 291.

Starters

Pan-Roasted Portobello Mushrooms with Three-Herb Gremolata

4 large fresh portobello mushrooms, about 1/4 lb (125 g) each, brushed clean and stem ends removed and trimmed

1/3 cup (2 oz/60 g) finely chopped yellow onion

1/2 cup (4 fl oz/120 ml) extra-virgin olive oil

Salt and freshly ground pepper

1/2 cup (3/4 oz/20 g) firmly packed fresh flat-leaf (Italian) parsley

1 tablespoon fresh thyme leaves, plus sprigs for garnish

1 teaspoon fresh rosemary leaves

2 cloves garlic, finely chopped

2 teaspoons finely chopped lemon zest, plus zest strips for garnish

1 small head radicchio, cored and quartered lengthwise

1 teaspoon red wine vinegar

Preheat the oven to 400°F (200°C). Finely chop the stems from the mushrooms, place in a bowl with the onion, and set aside. Arrange the mushroom caps, rounded sides up, on a large baking dish. Brush with 1/4 cup (2 fl oz/60 ml) of the olive oil and season with salt and pepper. Roast until lightly browned, about 15 minutes.

Meanwhile, finely chop together the parsley, thyme leaves, rosemary, garlic, and the 2 teaspoons lemon zest and add to the onion and mushroom mixture. In another bowl, cover the radicchio with cold water and let soak for 20–30 minutes to crisp. Drain well, slice thinly, and set aside.

Reduce the oven temperature to 350°F (180°C). Remove the mushrooms from the oven, turn over, and sprinkle with salt and pepper. Spoon the herb mixture into the center of the mushrooms, dividing evenly, and drizzle with 2 tablespoons of the remaining oil.

Continue to roast until the mushrooms are tender and the filling is softened, 10–15 minutes longer. Turn the mushrooms over again and bake about 5 minutes longer.

Meanwhile, in a large sauté pan over medium heat, warm the remaining 2 tablespoons olive oil. Add the radicchio and toss until heated through, about 2 minutes. Remove from the heat, add the vinegar, salt and pepper to taste, and toss to blend.

Divide the radicchio among individual plates and top with a portobello mushroom, smooth side up. Spoon the herb filling over the mushrooms, dividing evenly. Garnish with the thyme sprigs and strips of lemon zest, and serve immediately.

Serves 4

Grilled Lamb Kabobs with Mint-Yogurt Sauce

Kabobs are made all over the eastern Mediterranean, where lamb is the meat of choice. If you like, tuck the meat into pita wedges, and drizzle with the sauce. Grilled vegetables are a delicious addition and can be slipped into the pita as well.

To make the mint-yogurt sauce, line a fine-mesh sieve with cheesecloth (muslin) and place over a bowl. Spoon the yogurt into the sieve. Cover and refrigerate for 2 hours to drain.

In a small bowl, combine the drained yogurt, olive oil, chopped mint, garlic, and lemon juice. Stir to mix well. Season to taste with salt and pepper. Set aside.

Prepare a medium-hot fire for direct-heat cooking in a charcoal grill (see pages 8–9). Position the grill rack 4–5 inches (10–13 cm) above the fire. At the same time, put 6 bamboo skewers in water to cover for 30 minutes.

In a bowl, combine the lamb and the 2 tablespoons of the olive oil. Season with salt and pepper. Toss to coat evenly. Let stand until the coals are ready.

Drain the skewers and thread the lamb pieces onto them, dividing them evenly. Place on the grill rack and grill until browned on the first side, about 5 minutes. Turn the kabobs and continue to grill until browned on the second side and done to your liking, 4–5 minutes longer for medium-rare.

Transfer the kabobs to a serving platter, season with salt and pepper, and drizzle the yogurt sauce over the top. Garnish with the lemon wedges and mint sprigs. Serve immediately, warm, or at room temperature.

Serves 6

FOR THE MINT-YOGURT SAUCE:

3/4 cup (6 oz/185 g) plain yogurt

1 tablespoon extra-virgin olive oil

3 tablespoons chopped fresh mint, plus sprigs for garnish

1 clove garlic, minced

3 tablespoons lemon juice

1 lb (500 g) lamb cut from the leg, shoulder, or loin, trimmed of fat and cut into 1-inch (2.5-cm) pieces

2 tablespoons extra-virgin olive oil

Salt and freshly ground pepper

6 lemon wedges

Roast Asparagus Salad with Chèvre

This pretty salad is an ideal starter for a spring dinner, or a lovely light lunch dish. Pass hot, seed-crusted semolina or whole-grain bread at the table for mopping up extra dressing from the plate.

Olive oil for brushing

1½ lb (750 g) fat asparagus

Coarse salt and freshly ground pepper

About ½ teaspoon extra-virgin olive oil

FOR THE DRESSING:

2 tablespoons lemon juice

2 tablespoons extra-virgin olive oil

2 tablespoons pure olive oil

1 tablespoon Dijon mustard

3–4 tablespoons snipped fresh chives

Freshly ground pepper to taste

6 green (spring) onions, including about 2 inches (5 cm) of the green tops, chopped

7–8 cups (7–8 oz/220–250 g) mixed baby salad greens

2 cups (12 oz/375 g) cherry tomatoes, stems removed

¼ lb (125 g) herbed chèvre, cut into 6 slices

Preheat the oven to 400°F (200°C). Line a rimmed baking sheet with aluminum foil and brush with olive oil.

Snap off any tough ends from the asparagus spears and trim the break with a sharp knife. Using a vegetable peeler, and starting just below the tip, peel the skin off each spear, down to the end. Arrange the spears in a single layer on the prepared pan, season with salt and pepper, and drizzle with the extra-virgin olive oil. Roast until tender, 12–14 minutes. Transfer to a plate and set aside.

To make the dressing, in a small bowl, whisk together the lemon juice, extra-virgin olive oil, pure olive oil, and mustard. Stir in the chives, and season with pepper.

Spoon about 2 tablespoons of the dressing over the asparagus and let stand while tossing the salad.

In a large bowl, gently toss together the green onions and the salad greens. Add the tomatoes. Drizzle just enough of the dressing onto the salad for the greens to glisten, and toss again. (You may not need to use all of the dressing.) Immediately mound the salad in the center of large individual salad plates. Place a slice of chèvre on top of each mound of greens, and arrange asparagus spears around the perimeter of each plate, dividing them equally. Drizzle a few extra drops of the remaining dressing over the chèvre. Serve immediately.

Serves 6

Roasted Peppers with Anchovies

Serve this robust Italian dish with bread or on an antipasto platter. Canned anchovies vary greatly, as do people's appreciation of them. Use as many fillets from the can as you like, or even all of them.

To roast the peppers, preheat a broiler (grill). Cut the bell peppers in half lengthwise and remove the stems and seeds. Place, cut sides down, on a baking sheet. Broil (grill) until the skins blacken and blister. Remove from the broiler, drape the peppers loosely with aluminum foil, and let cool for 10 minutes, then peel away the skins. Cut lengthwise into strips $1/3$ inch (9 mm) wide. (This technique also works well for large, firm, fresh chiles, such as poblano chiles.)

Place the pepper strips in a large bowl. Add the olive oil, $1^{1}/2$ tablespoons red wine vinegar, and the garlic. Drain as many anchovy fillets as desired (see note) and finely mince them. Add to the pepper strips and season with salt. The pepper mixture can be prepared up to this point several hours in advance and stored at room temperature.

Stir in the parsley and adjust the seasonings just before serving, adding a splash more vinegar if needed.

Serves 4–6

6 large, thick-walled
bell peppers (capsicums),
preferably 2 *each* red, yellow,
and green

2½ tablespoons extra-virgin
olive oil

1½ tablespoons red wine
vinegar, or more as needed

1 large clove garlic, minced

1 can (2 oz/60 g) anchovy
fillets in olive oil

Salt

2 tablespoons minced fresh
flat-leaf (Italian) parsley

Chicken Souvlaki

Visitors to Greece will find chicken, pork, lamb, and beef souvlaki served at both streetside stands and restaurant tables. They are terrific straight from the skewer with just a squeeze of lemon, or stuffed into pita bread with the Mint–Yogurt Sauce (page 17).

In a bowl, stir together the olive oil, wine, lemon juice, onion, garlic, bay leaves, oregano, and salt and pepper to taste. Add the chicken pieces and turn to coat evenly. Cover and refrigerate for at least 1 hour or up to overnight.

Prepare a medium-hot fire for direct-heat cooking in a charcoal grill (see pages 8–9). Position a grill rack 4–5 inches (10–13 cm) above the fire. At the same time, put 6 bamboo skewers in water to cover for 30 minutes.

Remove the chicken pieces from the marinade and drain the skewers. Thread the chicken pieces onto the skewers, dividing the pieces evenly among them. Place the skewers on the grill rack and grill, turning once, until the chicken is opaque throughout when pierced with a knife, 3–4 minutes on each side. Season to taste with salt and pepper.

Transfer the chicken skewers to a warmed platter and garnish with lemon wedges and parsley. Serve immediately.

Serves 6

3 tablespoons extra-virgin olive oil

2 tablespoons dry white wine

1 tablespoon lemon juice

1/4 cup (1 1/2 oz/45 g) minced yellow onion

1 clove garlic, minced

2 bay leaves, broken or chopped into tiny pieces

1 teaspoon dried oregano

Salt and freshly ground pepper

1 lb (500 g) skinless, boneless chicken, cut into 1-inch (2.5-cm) pieces

Lemon wedges

Flat-leaf (Italian) parsley leaves

Rice Stick Noodles with Grilled Pork

1 lb (500 g) boneless pork loin

¼ cup (2 oz/60 g) sugar

1 teaspoon lemon juice

½ teaspoon freshly ground pepper

2 shallots, finely minced

2 tablespoons peanut or corn oil

1½ teaspoons soy sauce

1½ teaspoons fish sauce

1 lb (500 g) dried rice stick noodles

4 tablespoons (⅓ oz/10 g) coarsely chopped fresh mint

4 tablespoons (⅓ oz/10 g) fresh cilantro (fresh coriander)

Garlic-Lime Dipping Sauce (page 290)

1 cup (5 oz/155 g) finely julienned peeled cucumber

1 carrot, peeled and finely julienned

1 fresh red serrano chile, seeded and finely sliced

1 cup (3 oz/90 g) finely shredded red cabbage

¼ cup (1 oz/30 g) coarsely chopped roasted peanuts

Enclose the pork in plastic wrap and place in a freezer until partially frozen, about 1 hour. Meanwhile, in a small, heavy saucepan over medium heat, combine the sugar and ⅓ cup (3 fl oz/80 ml) cold water. Bring to a boil, and cook just until large, deep brown bubbles form, 5–8 minutes. Remove from the heat and stir in ¼ cup (2 fl oz/60 ml) hot water. Place over medium-high heat and cook, stirring constantly, until a light syrup forms that coats the back of a spoon, about 3 minutes longer. Remove from the heat, add the lemon juice and pepper, and pour into a large bowl; let cool. Stir in the shallots, oil, soy sauce, and fish sauce.

Cut the pork across the grain into thin slices, then into strips 1 inch (2.5 cm) wide. Place between 2 sheets of plastic wrap. Using a meat pounder, pound the strips until flattened. Add to the sugar mixture, cover and refrigerate for 20 minutes.

Cook the rice noodles according to the package directions. Drain, rinse with cold running water, and drain again thoroughly; set aside.

Prepare a medium-hot fire for direct–heat cooking in a grill (see pages 8–9). Position a grill rack 4–6 inches (10–15 cm) above the fire.

Divide 2 tablespoons each of the mint and cilantro among 6 bowls. Drizzle each with 1 tablespoon dipping sauce. Divide the noodles among the bowls and top with equal amounts of the cucumber, carrot, chile, and cabbage and the remaining mint and cilantro. Cover and refrigerate.

Oil the grill rack, lay the pork strips flat directly on the rack, and grill, turning once, until marked with grill lines, about 2 minutes on each side. Divide the pork strips among the bowls. Sprinkle with the peanuts, drizzle with the remaining dipping sauce, and serve immediately.

Serves 6

Prosciutto-Stuffed Figs

The saltiness of prosciutto and the sweetness of figs make a rich yet light appetizer that perfectly complements grilled meat. Figs are in season from summer through early fall, the perfect time of year to serve this Mediterranean-inspired first course.

Using a sharp knife, cut down through the top of each fig, cutting only three-fourths of the way through the fruit.

Gather first 1 slice and then a second slice of the prosciutto and tuck them into the center of a fig, letting the meat spill out over the top. Repeat until all the figs are stuffed. Sprinkle evenly with the pepper.

Divide the greens evenly among 6 individual plates. Top each with 2 stuffed figs and serve.

Serves 6

12 soft, ripe green or black figs such as Mission, Adriatic, or Kadota

24 thin slices prosciutto, about 1/4 lb (125 g) total weight

1/2 teaspoon freshly ground pepper

3 cups (3 oz/90 g) arugula (rocket) or baby lettuces

Grilled Shrimp Mousse on Sugarcane Sticks

For this Vietnamese starter, sugarcane skewers are wrapped with shrimp mousse, steamed, and then grilled. The hot shrimp is pulled off the sugarcane, wrapped in a lettuce leaf with herbs and cucumber, and enjoyed with a tangy dipping sauce.

2 egg whites

2 large shallots, quartered

2 cloves garlic

1 green (spring) onion, white part only, chopped

1 tablespoon fish sauce

1 teaspoon sugar

1 teaspoon cornstarch (cornflour)

1/2 teaspoon salt

1/4 teaspoon ground pepper

1 lb (500 g) medium shrimp (prawns), peeled and deveined

3 pieces fresh or canned sugarcane, each about 6 inches (15 cm) long

12 red-leaf or butter (Boston) lettuce leaves

12 sprigs fresh cilantro (fresh coriander)

36 fresh mint leaves

1 small English (hothouse) cucumber, halved lengthwise and thinly sliced

Garlic-Lime Dipping Sauce (page 290)

Beat the egg whites until frothy and set aside. In a food processor, combine the shallots, garlic, and green onion and process until finely minced. Add the fish sauce, sugar, cornstarch, salt, and pepper; pulse once or twice to mix. Add the shrimp and process until puréed, 5–10 seconds. Scrape down the sides of the bowl and add the egg whites; pulse a few times to combine.

Oil a baking sheet. Quarter the sugarcane sticks lengthwise. With wet hands, shape 2 tablespoons of the shrimp purée into an oblong ball. Mold the purée around the middle of a length of sugarcane, leaving 1 1/2 inches (4 cm) uncovered at each end. Set on the prepared sheet. Repeat the molding process with the remaining shrimp purée and sugarcane.

Prepare a hot fire for direct-heat cooking in a grill (see pages 8–9). Position the grill rack 4–6 inches (10–15 cm) above the fire. Arrange the lettuce leaves, cilantro sprigs, mint leaves, and cucumber slices on a serving platter.

Bring a wok half full of water to a boil. Oil the bottom of a bamboo steamer basket or a heatproof plate. Arrange the sugarcane sticks in the basket or on the plate without touching. Set in the wok, cover, and cook until the shrimp is opaque throughout, 4–5 minutes. Steam in batches if necessary. If using a plate, pat the sugarcane sticks with paper towels to remove excess moisture.

Oil the grill rack, set the sticks diagonally across the rack, and grill, turning occasionally, until golden brown, 3–5 minutes. Serve hot with the dipping sauce.

Serves 6

Grilled Eggplant with Mung Bean Noodles

2 oz (60 g) dried mung bean noodles

4 Asian (slender) eggplants (aubergines), about 6 inches (15 cm) long, or 1 globe eggplant, about 1¼ lb (625 g)

Peanut oil for brushing

Asian Dressing (page 290)

1 tablespoon sesame seeds

1 small English (hothouse) cucumber, peeled and cut into thin strips 2 inches (5 cm) long

1 green (spring) onion, including the tender green tops, minced

2 tablespoons coarsely chopped fresh cilantro (fresh coriander)

Place the noodles in a bowl, add water to cover, and soak until soft and pliable, about 15 minutes. Drain. Bring a large pot three-fourths full of water to a boil. Add the noodles and cook until plump and transparent, about 3 minutes. Drain, rinse with cold running water, and drain again. Using kitchen scissors, cut the mound of noodles in 4 or 5 places to create smaller pieces. Place in a large bowl, cover, and refrigerate for about 30 minutes.

Prepare a hot fire for direct-heat cooking in a grill (see pages 8–9). Position the grill rack 4–6 inches (10–15 cm) above the fire.

Cut the eggplants lengthwise into slices ¼ inch (6 mm) thick. Brush both sides with peanut oil. Place the slices directly on the grill rack. Cook, turning once, until tender and marked with grill lines, about 2 minutes per side. Transfer to a plate. Let cool, then cut the eggplant into strips 2 inches (5 cm) long. Transfer to a bowl, cover, and refrigerate for about 30 minutes.

Pour the dressing over the eggplant and mix well. Add the dressed eggplant to the bowl with the mung bean noodles. Top with the sesame seeds, cucumber strips, green onions, and cilantro, and serve.

Serves 4

Tandoori Chicken Wings with Raita

Place the wings in a large nonaluminum bowl and sprinkle with the lime juice.

In a food processor, combine the yogurt, garlic, ginger, paprika, salt, cumin, coriander, turmeric, and allspice. Process until smooth. Pour over the chicken wings, then turn to coat. Cover and refrigerate for 24 hours. Remove from the refrigerator 30 minutes before grilling.

To make the raita, place the cucumbers in a sieve set over a bowl and sprinkle with the salt, vinegar, and sugar. Let stand for 15 minutes. Press lightly with the back of a wooden spoon to release the excess liquid, then transfer to a clean bowl. Add the yogurt and chives, mix well, cover, and refrigerate until serving.

Prepare a hot fire for direct-heat cooking in a covered grill (see pages 8–9). Position the grill rack 4–6 inches (10–15 cm) above the fire.

Lightly oil a hinged grill basket. Remove the chicken wings from the marinade and place in the basket. Set the basket on the grill rack, cover the grill, and open the vents. Cook, turning once, until the skin is crisp and the juices run clear when a wing is pierced, about 25 minutes total. If it seems like the wings are browning too quickly, close the vents to restrict the airflow.

Transfer to a warmed platter and serve hot. Pass the raita at the table.

Serves 4

3 lb (1.5 kg) chicken wings

Juice of 1 lime

1/2 cup (4 oz/125 g) plain yogurt

2 cloves garlic, chopped

1 teaspoon peeled and minced fresh ginger

1 tablespoon paprika

2 teaspoons salt

1/2 teaspoon ground cumin

1/2 teaspoon ground coriander

1/4 teaspoon ground turmeric

Pinch of ground allspice

FOR THE RAITA:

2 cucumbers, peeled, halved, seeded, and finely chopped

1/2 teaspoon salt

1/2 teaspoon red wine vinegar

1/4 teaspoon sugar

1/2 cup (4 oz/125 g) plain yogurt

1 teaspoon snipped fresh chives

Roasted Beet and Wilted Beet Greens Salad with Orange Vinaigrette

If the beet leaves are not fresh and tender, substitute 2 or 3 bunches of arugula (rocket). Rinse the arugula and trim away the tough stems. It is not necessary to cook the arugula leaves. Simply toss with the dressing and top with the beet wedges.

6 bunches beets with leafy green tops, about 3 lb (1.5 kg) total weight

1 teaspoon salt

FOR THE ORANGE VINAIGRETTE:

1/3 cup (3 fl oz/80 ml) extra-virgin olive oil

3 tablespoons red wine vinegar

2 teaspoons finely grated orange zest

Salt and freshly ground pepper

1/2 sweet onion such as Vidalia, cut-crosswise into thin slices

6 thin navel orange slices, halved

Snipped fresh chives (optional)

Preheat the oven to 350°F (180°C). Trim off the beet greens, leaving about 1/2 inch (12 mm) of the stems intact; reserve the leaves. Rinse the beets well but do not peel. Wrap each beet tightly in a piece of heavy-duty aluminum foil; double fold the edges so the juices won't leak out. Place directly on the center oven rack. Roast until tender when pierced with a skewer, 45–55 minutes.

Meanwhile, trim the long stems from the beet greens and reserve only the leaves that are free of blemishes, discarding the others. Rinse thoroughly and dry well. Gather the leaves together and cut crosswise into strips 1 inch (2.5 cm) wide.

Half fill a saucepan with water and bring to a boil over high heat. Add the beet greens and salt and cook, uncovered, until the greens are tender, about 8 minutes. Drain well and set aside.

When the beets are ready, remove them from the oven and leave wrapped in the foil until cool enough to handle, about 1 hour. Then, carefully remove the foil and rub off the skins. If there are beet juices in the foil, place the juices in a small bowl.

To make the vinaigrette, add the olive oil, vinegar, orange zest, and salt and pepper to taste to any beet juices in the small bowl. Whisk to blend.

Cut the beets into wedges. In a large bowl, combine the beets, onion, cooked beet greens, and dressing. Toss to mix.

Divide the salad among individual plates. Garnish each plate with 2 orange slice halves and snipped chives, if using. Serve immediately.

Serves 6

Grilled Asparagus with Smoked Salmon and Tarragon Mayonnaise

Asparagus takes readily to brief grilling, which adds a mild smoky undertone to the vegetable's nutty, sweet flavor. Combined with smoked salmon, grilled asparagus is a singular beginning to a Sunday brunch or a candlelit dinner.

Prepare a hot fire for direct-heat cooking in a grill (see pages 8–9). Position the grill rack 4–6 inches (10–15 cm) above the fire.

To make the tarragon mayonnaise, place the mayonnaise in a small bowl. Add the tarragon, lemon juice, oil, and salt and mix well. Cover and refrigerate until ready to serve.

Break off any tough stem ends from the asparagus, then trim the ragged ends with a knife. Bring a frying pan three-fourths full of water to a boil. Add the asparagus and parboil for 2 minutes. Drain, rinse with cold running water until cool, then drain again.

Place the asparagus directly on the grill rack or in a grill basket on the rack and grill, turning as needed, until lightly marked with grill lines and just tender, 2–3 minutes on each side.

To serve, make a bed of the smoked salmon slices on 4 individual plates, dividing the salmon evenly. Arrange the grilled asparagus on top of the salmon along with some tarragon mayonnaise, again dividing evenly. Garnish with the lemon wedges and serve immediately.

Serves 4

FOR THE TARRAGON MAYONNAISE:

3/4 cup (6 fl oz/180 ml) mayonnaise

1/4 cup (1/3 oz/10 g) minced fresh tarragon

1 teaspoon lemon juice

1 teaspoon extra-virgin olive oil

1/4 teaspoon salt

1 1/2 lb (750 g) asparagus

1/2 lb (250 g) smoked salmon, thinly sliced

1 lemon, cut into wedges

Baked Radicchio with Prosciutto

This warm and rustic antipasto is a study in contrasts, with the crisp salty-sweet proscuitto complementing the mildly bitter, tender radicchio. Accompany the dish with a chilled white wine and scatter a few olives alongside each serving, if you like.

2 heads radicchio, about ¾ lb (375 g) each

2 tablespoons olive oil

12 large, thin slices prosciutto, about ⅛ lb (60g)

Lemon wedges

Preheat the oven to 400°F (200°C). Oil a baking sheet.

Cut each radicchio head into 6 wedges through the stem end. Brush each wedge lightly with olive oil. Wrap each wedge with a slice of prosciutto, then arrange on the prepared baking sheet and turn to coat the prosciutto with the oil.

Bake until the radicchio is tender and the prosciutto begins to crisp, 12–14 minutes. Transfer to a platter and serve with lemon wedges.

Serves 6

Grilled Summer Heirloom Vegetables with Black Bean Salsa

Pick over the beans and discard any damaged beans or impurities. Rinse, place in a bowl, and add water to cover generously. Let soak for 3 hours.

Drain the beans and place in a saucepan along with the stock, yellow onion, carrot, and celery. Bring to a boil, then reduce the heat to low and simmer, uncovered, until tender but not mushy, about 1 hour.

Meanwhile, bring a saucepan three-fourths full of water to a boil, add the corn, and blanch for 30 seconds. Drain and set aside.

When the beans are ready, drain and rinse in cold water to cool, then drain again and place in a bowl. Add the olive oil and toss well. Add the green onion, bell pepper, garlic, jalapeño chile, and corn and toss again. Season with the cumin and salt and pepper to taste. Sprinkle with the cilantro. Set aside, allowing the flavors to come together, until ready to serve.

Prepare a hot fire for direct-heat cooking in a grill (see pages 8–9). Position the grill rack about 4 inches (10 cm) above the fire. At the same time, put 8 bamboo skewers in water to cover for 30 minutes. Lightly brush the grill rack with olive oil. Alternatively, preheat a broiler (grill).

Drain the skewers. Thread the red onion, eggplant, zucchini, fennel, mushrooms, tomatoes, and garlic onto the skewers, alternating them and dividing them evenly. Place the skewers on the grill rack or on a broiler pan. Brush lightly with olive oil, and season with salt and pepper. Grill or broil, turning as needed, until lightly browned, about 10 minutes. Transfer the skewers to a serving platter. Serve with the salsa.

Serves 4

1¹⁄₈ cups (8 oz/250 g) dried black beans

3 cups (24 fl oz/750 ml) Vegetable Stock (page 288) or broth

¹⁄₂ cup (2¹⁄₂ oz/75 g) finely chopped yellow onion

1 carrot, peeled and diced

1 celery stalk, sliced

1 cup (6 oz/185 g) corn kernels

1 tablespoon olive oil, plus more for brushing

¹⁄₂ cup (1¹⁄₂ oz/45 g) thinly sliced green (spring) onion

1 red bell pepper (capsicum), diced

2 cloves garlic, minced

1 jalapeño chile, minced

1 teaspoon ground cumin

Salt and freshly ground pepper

¹⁄₂ cup (¹⁄₂ oz/15 g) fresh cilantro (fresh coriander) leaves

1 red onion, cut into wedges

1 *each* Asian (slender) eggplant (aubergine) and zucchini (courgette), sliced

1 fennel bulb, trimmed and cut lengthwise into 8 wedges

8 cremini mushrooms, stemmed

8 cherry tomatoes

16 cloves garlic, peeled

Grilled Bread with Ripe Tomatoes and Olive Oil

During tomato season, Spanish cooks prepare this simple dish of ripe tomatoes, fragrant oil, and country bread. Use air-cured Serrano ham for the most traditional flavor, although Italian prosciutto or French Bayonne ham can be substituted.

2 cloves garlic

Salt

¼ cup (2 fl oz/60 ml) extra-virgin olive oil

12 slices coarse country bread, each about ¾ inch (2 cm) thick

3 large, very ripe tomatoes (about 2 lb), halved crosswise

Freshly ground pepper

FOR THE OPTIONAL GARNISHES:

½ cup (2½ oz/75g) green or black brine-cured olives, pitted and slivered

6 paper-thin slices serrano ham

12 paper-thin slices manchego cheese

Prepare a medium-hot fire for direct-heat cooking in a charcoal grill (see pages 8–9). Position the grill rack 4–5 inches (10–13 cm) above the fire.

In a mortar, combine the garlic and salt to taste. Mash together with a pestle to form a paste. Mix in the olive oil.

Place the bread slices on the grill rack and grill, turning once, until golden brown, 30–60 seconds on each side. Transfer the bread slices to a platter.

Cupping a tomato half in your palm, rub it over the top sides of 2 pieces of grilled bread, squeezing slightly to leave a smear of pulp, seeds, and juice on the surface. Repeat with the remaining tomato halves and bread. Drizzle the olive oil–garlic mixture evenly over the bread slices and sprinkle with pepper. Serve immediately with the optional garnishes arranged on top, if desired.

Serves 6

Spicy Pork Kabobs with Moorish Flavors

The Moors invaded Spain in the eighth century and remained for 500 years. Of Berber and Arab descent, they left their influence on every aspect of Spanish life, including the kitchen. This recipe shows their legacy in its heavy use of spices.

In a mortar, combine the garlic with $1/2$ teaspoon of the salt. Mash together with a pestle to form a paste. In a dry frying pan over high heat, combine the coriander seeds, paprika, cumin seeds, thyme, and red pepper flakes. Heat, shaking the pan occasionally, until hot and fragrant, about 30 seconds. Transfer the mixture to a spice grinder and grind to a fine powder.

In a bowl, stir together the garlic paste, the ground spices, the remaining $1/2$ teaspoon salt, the black pepper to taste, olive oil, lemon juice, and parsley. Add the pork cubes and turn to coat well. Cover and let stand at cool room temperature for 2 hours, stirring occasionally.

Prepare a medium-hot fire for direct-heat cooking in a charcoal grill (see pages 8–9). Position the grill rack 4–5 inches (10–13 cm) above the fire. At the same time, put 12 bamboo skewers in water to cover for 30 minutes.

Remove the pork cubes from the marinade, reserving the marinade, and drain the skewers. Thread the pork cubes onto the skewers, dividing the cubes evenly among them. In a small saucepan, bring the reserved marinade to a boil over high heat and boil for about 3 minutes. Remove from the heat. Place the kabobs on the grill rack and grill, basting occasionally with the reserved marinade and turning every 2–3 minutes, until browned but still juicy, 10–15 minutes.

Transfer to a warmed platter and garnish with lemon wedges. Serve immediately.

Serves 6

2 cloves garlic, thinly sliced

1 teaspoon salt

1 teaspoon coriander seeds

1 teaspoon paprika

3/4 teaspoon cumin seeds

1/2 teaspoon dried thyme

1/4 teaspoon red pepper flakes

Freshly ground black pepper

3 tablespoons olive oil

1 tablespoon lemon juice

1 tablespoon chopped fresh flat-leaf (Italian) parsley

1 lb (500 g) lean pork, cut into 3/4–1-inch (2–2.5-cm) cubes

Lemon wedges

Poultry

Chicken Kabobs with Lemon and Oregano

Cubes of chicken are threaded onto skewers with pieces of eggplant, bell pepper, and onion and then brushed with characteristic seasonings of the Greek Isles. Serve on a bed of rice pilaf and garnish, if you like, with a sprinkling of finely grated lemon zest.

½ cup (4 fl oz/125 ml) lemon juice

¼ cup (2 fl oz/60 ml) dry white wine

2 tablespoons olive oil

2 cloves garlic, minced

2 tablespoons chopped fresh oregano

Grated zest of ½ lemon

Salt and freshly ground pepper

1½ lb (750 g) skinless, boneless chicken breasts or thighs, cut into 1½-inch (4-cm) cubes

1 Asian (slender) eggplant (aubergine), cut crosswise into slices

1 red bell pepper (capsicum), seeded and cut into 1-inch (2.5-cm) squares

1 yellow onion, halved, separated into layers, and then cut into 1½-inch (4-cm) squares

1 lemon, cut into 8 wedges

In a large bowl, combine the lemon juice, wine, oil, garlic, oregano, lemon zest, and salt and pepper to taste. Stir in the chicken, eggplant, bell pepper, and onion. Cover and marinate in the refrigerator for 1 hour.

Meanwhile, prepare a hot fire for indirect–heat cooking in a covered grill (see pages 8–9). Place the grill rack 4–6 inches (10–15 cm) above the fire. At the same time, put 8 wooden skewers in water to cover and let stand for 30 minutes.

Drain the skewers and thread the chicken, eggplant, bell pepper, and onion pieces onto them, alternating the pieces and dividing them equally. Place on the perimeter of the grill rack directly over the fire. Grill, turning the skewers once or twice, until the chicken is browned, about 5 minutes total. Move the skewers to the center of the grill rack so they are not directly over the fire. Cover the grill, open the vents halfway, and cook, turning the skewers occasionally, until the chicken is opaque throughout and its juices run clear when the meat is pierced with a knife, and the vegetables are tender, 10–15 minutes longer.

Transfer the skewers to a warmed platter or individual plates and serve with the lemon wedges.

Serves 4

Roast Chicken Stuffed with Winter Savory and Preserved Lemons

To make the preserved lemons, pour 3 qt (3 l) water into a nonaluminum saucepan and bring to a boil. Add the lemons and return to a boil. Cook the lemons until softened, 3–4 minutes. Drain and immerse in cold water until cool enough to handle. Cut a shallow X in the bottom of each lemon.

In the same saucepan, combine 6 cups (48 fl oz/1.5 l) water, the salt, cinnamon sticks, coriander seeds, peppercorns, and cloves to make a brine. Bring to a boil. Remove from the heat.

Sterilize 2 wide-mouthed glass canning jars, each large enough to hold 4 or 5 lemons. Tightly pack the whole lemons into the sterilized jars. Pour in the 1 cup (8 fl oz/ 250 ml) olive oil, dividing it evenly, then pour in the hot brine, filling to within $^{1}/_{2}$ inch (12 mm) of the rim(s). If there is not enough brine, add more olive oil if necessary. Tap the jars on the work surface to remove any air bubbles. Seal the jars tightly. Store in a cool, dark place for at least 2 months or up to 6 months.

Preheat the oven to 350°F (180°C).

Rinse the chicken and pat dry with paper towels. Rub the surface of the chicken with a preserved lemon quarter, the salt, pepper, and the winter savory leaves. Stuff 4–5 winter savory sprigs and all but 3 of the remaining lemon quarters into the cavity of the chicken. Truss the chicken and place in a roasting pan.

Roast until an instant-read thermometer inserted into the thickest part of the thigh, away from the bone, registers 165°–170°F (74°–77°C), or until the juices run clear when a thigh joint is pierced with a knife, about 1$^{1}/_{4}$ hours.

Remove the chicken from the oven, cover loosely with aluminum foil, and let stand for 10 minutes. Garnish with preserved lemons and sprigs of winter savory, if you like. Carve into pieces and serve.

Serves 4

FOR THE PRESERVED LEMONS:

7–10 firm lemons

$^{2}/_{3}$ cup (5 oz/155 g) sea salt

2 cinnamon sticks

4 teaspoons coriander seeds

2 teaspoons peppercorns

8 whole cloves

1 cup (8 fl oz/250 ml) olive oil, plus more if needed

1 chicken, 2$^{1}/_{2}$–3 lb (1.25–1.5 kg)

3 or 4 preserved lemons (above), quartered lengthwise, plus more for garnish (optional)

1 teaspoon salt

1 teaspoon freshly ground pepper

1 tablespoon fresh winter savory leaves

4 or 5 sprigs winter savory, about 4 inches (10 cm) long; plus more for garnish (optional)

Thai Chicken Salad

Shredded chicken, diced avocado, and greens are dressed with the flavors of Southeast Asia to make a light main-course salad for the outdoor table. For a festive presentation, omit the diced avocado from the salad and spoon the salad into 4 avocado halves.

2 chicken breast halves, 1/2 lb (250 g) each

Salt and freshly ground pepper

1/2 small head green cabbage

1/2 small head iceberg lettuce

1/2 cup (4 fl oz/125 ml) unseasoned rice vinegar

3 tablespoons fish sauce

1/3 teaspoon Asian sesame oil

2 teaspoons sugar

2 tablespoons seeded and minced serrano chile

1 small avocado, pitted, peeled, and finely diced

1/2 cup (3/4 oz/20 g) chopped fresh cilantro (fresh coriander)

Preheat the oven to 350°F (180°C).

Place the chicken breast halves, skin side up, on a rack in a roasting pan. Sprinkle generously with salt and pepper. Roast until the juices run clear when the chicken is pierced to the bone with a knife, 30–35 minutes. Remove from the oven and let cool. Remove and discard the skin. Remove the chicken from the bone and cut into 1/2-inch (12-mm) slices.

Place the cabbage half on a cutting board and, using a large knife, slice it crosswise into the thinnest possible shreds. Measure out 2 cups (6 oz/185 g); reserve any leftover cabbage for another use. Cut and measure the lettuce in the same way. Set aside.

In a bowl, stir together the vinegar, fish sauce, sesame oil, and sugar. Add the chicken and stir to coat with the dressing. Add the cabbage, lettuce, and chile and toss to combine. Add the diced avocado and gently turn the salad to distribute the ingredients evenly. Divide the salad among 4 individual plates or bowls. Sprinkle with the cilantro and serve.

Serves 4

Chicken Satay with Coconut-Lime Curry Sauce

For a little extra heat and color, garnish the curry sauce with minced jalapeño chiles. Serve on a bed of warm couscous. If chicken tenders are unavailable, cut boneless, skinless chicken breasts into thin strips.

16 chicken tenders, about 1¹/₄ lb (625 g) total weight

1 tablespoon soy sauce

2 tablespoons peeled and minced fresh ginger

2 large cloves garlic, minced

2 teaspoons curry powder

1 cup (8 fl oz/250 ml) nonfat (skim) milk

1 tablespoon sugar

2 teaspoons arrowroot

2 tablespoons lime juice

1 teaspoon coconut extract (essence)

Salt

In a bowl, toss together the chicken and soy sauce. Cover and refrigerate for 1 hour. Meanwhile, soak 16 bamboo skewers in water to cover for at least 30 minutes.

Preheat a broiler (grill). Heat a saucepan over medium heat. Coat the pan with nonstick cooking spray. Add the ginger, garlic, and curry powder and sauté for 1 minute. Add the milk and sugar, stir well, and simmer for 5 minutes to blend the flavors.

In a small bowl, stir the arrowroot into 2 teaspoons water until dissolved. Whisk it into the curry mixture and simmer until thickened, about 2 minutes. Remove the sauce from the heat and whisk in the lime juice and coconut extract. Season to taste with salt. Keep warm.

Coat a baking sheet with nonstick cooking spray. Thread the chicken onto skewers and place the skewers in a single layer on the prepared baking sheet. Place under the broiler about 4 inches (10 cm) from the heat source. Broil (grill), turning once, until it is opaque throughout when chicken is pierced with a knife, about 3 minutes on each side.

Remove from the broiler. Arrange the skewers on warmed individual plates. Spoon the sauce over them and serve hot.

Serves 4

Chicken-and-Apple Sausages with Mustard Sauce

Roasting smoky-sweet sausages with onions and wine makes a hearty, savory dish that's perfect for a casual fall super. Serve with toasted slices of rye bread or mashed potatoes.

Preheat the oven to 425°F (220°C).

Using a sharp knife, make 3 or 4 slits in each sausage. Scatter the onion slices in a 9-inch (23-cm) baking dish or pie dish. Place the sausages directly on the onions, and pour $1/2$ cup (4 fl oz/125 ml) of the wine into the dish.

Roast, adding more wine if necessary to prevent scorching, until the sausages are browned and crisp, the onions are soft, and the wine is nearly evaporated, 25–30 minutes.

Meanwhile, make the mustard sauce: In a small, heatproof bowl set over (but not touching) barely simmering water, stir the cream cheese until warm and smooth. Remove from the heat and whisk in the Dijon mustard and the $1/2$ teaspoon dry mustard. Taste and add more dry mustard as needed. Transfer the mustard sauce to a small bowl.

Serve the sausages and onions from the baking dish. Pass the sauce at the table.

Serves 4

4 smoked chicken-and-apple sausages, or other fruit-flavored chicken or turkey sausages, about 3-4 oz (90–125 g) each

1 large Vidalia or red onion, sliced

$1/2$-$1/4$ cup (4-6 fl oz/125–180 ml) full-bodied red wine

FOR THE MUSTARD SAUCE:

3 oz (90 g) cream cheese

6 tablespoons (3 oz/90 g) Dijon mustard

$1/2$ teaspoon dry mustard, or to taste

Provençal Roasted Turkey Breast

1 carrot, peeled and chopped

1 celery stalk, chopped

2 small yellow onions, chopped

1 bone-in turkey breast, 5-6 lb (2.5-3 kg)

1 lemon, halved

Coarse salt and freshly ground pepper

FOR THE SEASONING PASTE:

4 shallots

1 generous cup (6 oz/185 g) pitted oil-cured black olives

1/2 cup (1/2 oz/15 g) firmly packed fresh flat-leaf (Italian) parsley leaves

1 tablespoon *herbes de Provence*

1/2 teaspoon freshly ground pepper

1 tablespoon olive oil

8-10 Vidalia or other sweet onions

Preheat the oven to 400°F (200°C). Scatter the chopped carrot and celery and 1 of the yellow onions in the bottom of a large roasting pan. Set a rack over the vegetables.

Rinse the turkey breast and pat dry with paper towels. Rub the inside with the lemon, sprinkle with salt and pepper to taste, and set aside.

To make the seasoning paste, in a food processor, combine the shallots, parsley, olives, *herbes de Provence*, and pepper. Pulse until evenly chopped but not smooth; set aside.

Carefully slide your fingers under the skin on the turkey breast, separating it from the flesh but leaving it attached on the sides. Spread the seasoning paste under the skin, in the wing sockets, and inside the cavity. Fill the cavity with the remaining chopped onion. Brush the skin with the olive oil and set the turkey breast, on one side, on the rack.

Roast until the skin is browned, 15–20 minutes. Turn the breast onto the opposite side and continue to roast until the skin on the second side is browned, 15–20 minutes. Reduce the oven temperature to 350°F (180°C), turn the breast right side up, and continue to roast, basting every 10 minutes with the pan juices during the last 30 minutes, until the skin is crisp and browned and the juices run clear when the meat is pierced at the thickest portion, or an instant-read thermometer registers 162°–165°F (72°–74°C), about 2 hours longer. If the turkey skin is browning too fast, tent the pan with aluminum foil. Meanwhile, cut the onions as directed for the Balsamic Vidalia Blossoms on page 255. Add the onions to the pan during the last 35–40 minutes and roast, basting with the pan juices as well, until tender.

Transfer the turkey breast to a cutting board, tent with aluminum foil, and let rest for 15 minutes before carving. Thinly slice turkey across the grain, and arrange on a warmed platter with the Vidalia onions and serve immediately.

Serves 8–10

Broiled Cornish Hen al Diavolo

The liberal use of pungent black pepper explains why Italians call this preparation "devil's style." Arranged on a bed of baby salad greens, the warm chicken releases well-seasoned juices that serve as a deliciously savory salad dressing.

Rinse each bird inside and out. Place breast side up on a cutting board and, using a heavy knife positioned inside each bird, cut down both sides of the backbone to separate it from the body. Discard the backbones or save it for making stock. Turn each bird skin side down and crack the breastbone with the knife so that the bird lies flat. Pat dry with paper towels.

Coat each bird evenly on both sides with the olive oil, pepper, and salt to taste. Place on a platter, cover, and refrigerate for 1 hour; bring to room temperature before cooking.

Position a rack about 8 inches (20 cm) from the broiler (grill), then set a broiler pan on the rack. Preheat the broiler for 5 minutes.

Set the bird on the broiler pan, skin side down. Brush with any seasoned oil remaining on the platter. Place under the broiler and broil (grill) until the juices sizzle and the skin on the legs begins to brown, about 12 minutes. Remove from the broiler and collect any drippings in the bottom of the pan. Turn the bird skin side up, baste with the pan drippings, and return to the broiler. Broil until the skin browns and blisters and the juices run clear when the thickest part of the thigh is pierced with a knife, about 8 minutes. Remove from the broiler.

Put the greens on two individual dinner plates. Top with the bird and arrange the tomato wedges alongside. Drizzle the greens and tomato with 1 tablespoon of drippings from the broiler pan. Garnish the plate with the lemon wedge, and be sure to squeeze the lemon over the bird and greens before eating.

Serves 2

2 Cornish hens or poussins, 1¼–1½ lb (625–750 g) each

3 tablespoons extra-virgin olive oil

2 teaspoons coarsely ground pepper

Salt

2 oz (120 g) mixed baby salad greens (about 4 handfuls)

2 small ripe tomatoes, cut into wedges, plus a few yellow pear tomatoes, halved (optional)

2 lemon wedges

Smoky and Spicy Chicken Breasts

The delicious advantage to roasting chicken breasts on a bed of ham is that the meat stays moist while picking up the smoky quality of the meat. Add as much jalapeño pepper jelly as you like to produce a glaze that delivers a little fire.

½ lb (250 g) baked smoked ham, in one piece

8 boneless chicken breast halves, 6–7 oz (185–220 g) each, with skin intact

Coarse salt and freshly ground pepper

2 teaspoons ground coriander

3 tablespoons spicy hot red or green jalapeño pepper jelly, or to taste

½ bunch fresh cilantro (fresh coriander)

2 jalapeño chiles, chopped

Preheat the oven to 400°F (200°C).

Cut the smoked ham into narrow julienne strips about ⅛ inch (3 mm) thick. Scatter the ham over the bottom of a baking dish large enough to hold the chicken in a single layer.

Rinse the chicken breast halves and pat dry with paper towels. Season both sides of each piece with salt and pepper to taste, then rub about ¼ teaspoon of the ground coriander on the skin of each piece. Place the chicken pieces, skin sides up, on top of the ham.

Roast, basting with the pan juices after the first 15 minutes, until the skin is crisp, about 35 minutes total.

Meanwhile, in a small saucepan over high heat, warm the jelly until it melts, about 45 seconds. Remove the chicken from the oven. Brush or spoon about 1 teaspoon of the jelly on top of the crisp skin of each chicken piece and return the chicken to the oven. Continue roasting until the skin is glazed and the juices run clear when the meat is pierced at the thickest point with a knife, about 5 minutes longer.

Serve the chicken directly from the baking dish. Garnish with cilantro and the chopped jalapeños.

Serves 8

Red-Hot Barbecued Chicken

Evocative of southern barbecue in Tennessee, Mississippi, and Georgia, this sweet-hot sauce is a perfect partner to chicken. The sauce can be made in advance and stored tightly covered in the refrigerator for up to 2 weeks.

Prepare a hot fire for indirect-heat cooking in a covered grill (see pages 8–9). Position a grill rack 4–6 inches (10–15 cm) above the fire.

Meanwhile, make the sauce: In a small saucepan over medium-high heat, combine the onion, garlic, ketchup, vinegar, brown sugar, mustard, hot-pepper sauce, and Worcestershire sauce. Bring to a boil, stirring often. Reduce the heat to low and simmer, uncovered, until the sauce is thick and the flavors are blended, about 15 minutes. Remove from the heat and let cool.

Rub the seasoning rub on the chicken pieces, coating evenly, and set aside until ready to grill.

Place the chicken on the perimeter of the grill rack directly over the fire. Grill, turning once, until seared on both sides with grill marks, about 2 minutes on each side. Transfer the chicken pieces to a large platter and spoon the sauce evenly over them. Return the chicken to the grill rack, positioning the pieces in the center of the grill rack so that they are not directly over the fire. Cover the grill, open the vents halfway, and cook, turning once, until the chicken is opaque throughout and the juices run clear when the meat is pierced with a knife, about 20 minutes for the breasts and wings and 25 minutes for the thighs and drumsticks. Serve hot or at room temperature.

Serves 4

FOR THE SPICY BARBECUE SAUCE:

1/2 yellow onion, chopped

2 cloves garlic, minced

1 cup (8 fl oz/250 ml) tomato ketchup

1/3 cup (3 fl oz/80 ml) red wine vinegar

1/4 cup (2 oz/60 g) firmly packed brown sugar

1 tablespoon prepared yellow mustard

1-2 teaspoons hot-pepper sauce such as Tabasco

1 teaspoon Worcestershire sauce

Seasoning Rub (page 290)

2 chicken breast halves, about 1/2 lb (250 g) each, skinned

2 chicken thighs, about 6 oz (185 g) each, skinned

2 chicken drumsticks, about 1/4 lb (125 g) each, skinned

2 chicken wings

Chicken with Mustard, Tarragon, Carrots, and Leeks

This dish represents the best of French home cooking, which frequently pairs chicken with tarragon. Try replacing the Dijon mustard and tarragon with honey mustard or use a mustard flavored with other minced herbs.

½ cup (4 fl oz/125 ml) Chicken Stock (page 288) or broth

½ cup (4 fl oz/125 ml) heavy (double) cream

1 tablespoon Dijon mustard

2 tablespoons minced fresh tarragon

Salt and freshly ground pepper

3 small leeks, white and pale green parts only, halved lengthwise and very thinly sliced

3 small carrots, peeled and very thinly sliced

4 skinless, boneless chicken breast halves, about 6 oz (185 g) each

Preheat the oven to 375°F (190°C).

In a bowl, whisk together the stock, cream, mustard, and tarragon until blended. Season to taste with salt and pepper. Mix together the leeks and carrots and spread them out on the bottom of a baking dish large enough to hold all of the chicken in a single layer. Spoon the broth-cream mixture over the vegetables. Cover tightly with aluminum foil and bake for 20 minutes.

Season the chicken breasts with salt and pepper. Carefully uncover the baking dish, place the chicken on the bed of vegetables, cover, and bake for 15 minutes. Uncover and bake until the chicken is opaque throughout and the juices run clear when the meat is pierced with a knife, about 5 minutes longer.

Transfer the chicken onto 4 warm shallow serving bowls and spoon the contents of the baking dish over and around the breasts. Serve immediately.

Serves 4

Chicken with Sage and Prosciutto

The pleasant taste of the sage permeates the chicken hot from the oven. Leftovers are delicious served cold the next day, when the distinctive flavor of the prosciutto emerges. Accompany with steamed brown rice.

Preheat the oven to 400°F (200°C).

Rinse the chicken pieces and pat dry with paper towels. Trim the excess fat from the prosciutto, then cut the slices to the dimensions of the chicken pieces.

Carefully slide your fingers under the skin on each chicken piece, separating it from the meat but leaving it attached on one side. Place a slice of prosciutto directly on the meat and top it with a sage leaf. Carefully pull the skin back in place, and press gently with your palm to secure it.

Arrange the chicken pieces in 1 or 2 shallow baking dishes or in a roasting pan large enough to hold them in a single layer. Brush the skin with the olive oil and season to taste with salt and pepper.

Roast until the skin is crisp and brown and the juices run clear when a thigh is pierced at the thickest part with a knife, about 55 minutes. Remove from the oven and let rest for 10 minutes before serving.

Transfer the chicken pieces to a warmed platter and garnish with sage sprigs. Serve immediately.

Serves 10–12

6 chicken breast halves, about 6 oz (185 g) each

6 chicken drumsticks, about 4 oz (125 g) each

6 chicken thighs, about 5 oz (155 g) each

18 thin slices prosciutto

18 fresh sage leaves, plus sage sprigs for garnish

1 1/2–2 tablespoons olive oil

Coarse salt and freshly ground pepper

Lemon-Scented Roast Chicken

1 chicken, 3¹/₂–4 lb (1.75–2 kg)

Salt and freshly ground pepper

4 rosemary sprigs

3 lemons

1 tablespoon olive oil

1¹/₃ cups (1 fl oz/320 ml) Chicken Stock (page 288) or broth

¹/₄ cup (2 fl oz/60 ml) heavy (double) cream, or as needed

Position an oven rack in the lower third of the oven and preheat to 375°F (190°C).

Rinse the chicken and remove the giblets and excess fat. Pat the cavity dry and season with salt and pepper. Place 2 or 3 rosemary sprigs and one whole lemon in the cavity and secure it closed with a skewer. Tuck the wing tips under the body, then cross the drumsticks and, using kitchen string, tie the legs tightly together. Place the chicken, breast side up, on a rack in a heavy roasting pan. Rub the olive oil over the entire surface of the chicken. Pour ¹/₃ cup (3 fl oz/80 ml) of the stock into the pan.

Roast for 45 minutes. Squeeze the juice of one lemon over the chicken, and then pour ¹/₃ cup (3 fl oz/80 ml) of the stock over the chicken. Continue to roast until the skin is golden brown and an instant-read thermometer inserted into the thickest part of the thigh, away from the bone, registers 180°F (82°C), or until the juices run clear when a thigh is pierced with a knife, about 45 minutes longer.

Transfer the chicken to a cutting board and cover loosely with aluminum foil. Skim off and discard the fat from the pan drippings. Pour the remaining ²/₃ cup (5 fl oz/160 ml) stock into the pan and place on the stovetop over medium heat. Deglaze the pan, stirring with a whisk to dislodge any brown bits from the pan bottom. Gradually whisk in the ¹/₄ cup (2 fl oz/60 ml) cream. Continue to whisk until the sauce thickens, about 2 minutes. If the sauce becomes too thick, thin with additional stock or cream.

Transfer the chicken to a warmed platter. Garnish with the remaining rosemary sprigs. Cut the remaining lemon into slices and arrange around the chicken. Pour the sauce into a warmed bowl and pass at the table. Carve the chicken and serve immediately.

Serves 4

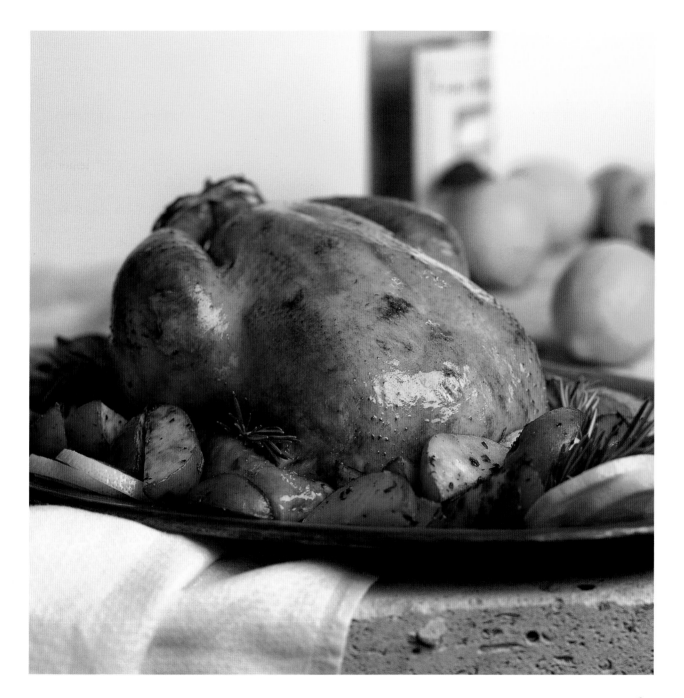

Turkey with Curried Apricot Glaze

Accompany this festive holiday offering with wild rice tossed with corn kernels and chopped green (spring) onions. For a slightly different but equally delicious flavor, dried cherries can be substituted for the cranberries in the glaze.

In a small bowl, combine the apricot preserves, vinegar, mustard, curry powder, and garlic. Stir to mix well and set aside.

Preheat a broiler (grill). Heat a large frying pan over medium heat. Coat the pan with nonstick cooking spray. Season the turkey with salt and pepper and add it to the pan. Cook the turkey until browned, about 5 minutes. Turn the turkey over and cover the pan. Cook until just opaque throughout, about 5 minutes longer. Remove from the heat.

Arrange the turkey tenderloins on a baking sheet. Spoon 1 tablespoon of the apricot mixture over each tenderloin. Slip under the broiler about 4 inches (10 cm) from the heat source and broil for 2 minutes. Mix the cranberries into the remaining apricot mixture and spoon over the turkey, dividing it evenly. Continue to broil until the turkey is well glazed, about 2 minutes longer.

Transfer the turkey tenderloins to a work surface. Let rest for 7 minutes. Slice the turkey on the diagonal and divide among warmed individual plates, fanning the slices. Serve hot.

Serves 4

1/4 cup (2 1/2 oz/75 g) apricot preserves

2 tablespoons white wine vinegar

2 1/2 teaspoons Dijon mustard

2 1/2 teaspoons curry powder

1 teaspoon minced garlic

3 turkey tenderloins, 1/2 lb (250 g) each

Salt and freshly ground pepper

1 1/2 tablespoons dried cranberries

Chicken and Vegetable Kabobs

These easy kabobs have a bright Mediterranean flavor, tempered by the smoky flavor of cumin. Serve them with tabbouleh or with pita bread as a weekend lunch. If you do not have yellow or red bell peppers on hand, substitute green bell peppers.

1 small lemon

1/3 cup olive oil

1 large garlic clove

1/4 teaspoon ground cumin

1/4 teaspoon dried thyme

1/4 teaspoon salt

1/8 teaspoon freshly ground pepper

4 skinless, boneless chicken breast halves

1 small yellow or red bell pepper (capsicum), stem and seeds removed, cut into 4 equal chunks

1 small red onion, peeled and cut into 8 wedges

Cut the lemon in half crosswise and squeeze the juice into a large glass bowl. Add the olive oil. Press the garlic into the bowl. Add the cumin, thyme, salt, and pepper and mix well. Set aside.

With a small, sharp knife, cut each chicken breast half lengthwise into 4 strips. Put in the bowl with the lemon mixture and stir to coat the chicken.

Preheat the broiler (grill).

Remove the chicken from the marinade. Reserve the marinade. Divide the chicken and the vegetables into 4 equal portions. Thread the portions, alternating the chicken pieces with the vegetable pieces, onto 4 metal skewers, weaving each chicken strip through the skewer 2 or 3 times. Do not pack the foods too tightly.

Place the skewers on the broiler pan and brush the kabobs with the leftover marinade. Place under the broiler about 4–6 inches (10–15 cm) from the heat source and broil (grill) until browned on one side, 5–10 minutes. Turn the kabobs and broil until browned on the second side, and the juices run clear when the meat is pierced with a knife, 5–10 minutes. Serve immediately.

Serves 4

Roast Chicken with Spinach-Rice Stuffing

Preheat the oven to 350°F (180°C). Remove the tough stems from the spinach, place in a nonstick saucepan, and add 3 tablespoons water. Cover and cook over high heat, turning the leaves as needed, until wilted, about 3 minutes. Drain and let cool, then press out the excess liquid. Chop the leaves.

In a frying pan over medium heat, melt the butter. Add the onion and mushrooms and sauté until softened, about 3 minutes. Stir in the garlic and herbs and sauté for about 20 seconds longer. Add the spinach and cook, stirring, until the flavors are blended, about 2 minutes. Remove from the heat and let cool. In a bowl, combine the rice and ricotta and mix well. Stir in the spinach mixture, then mix in the egg. Season to taste with salt and pepper. Stir in the pine nuts.

Rinse the chicken and pat dry with paper towels. Stuff loosely with the rice mixture. Using kitchen string, tie the drumsticks together. Tuck the wing tips under the body. Butter a baking dish, put the remaining stuffing in it, and cover with aluminum foil.

To make the herb paste, in a small bowl, combine the oil, garlic, paprika, tarragon, and parsley. Mix to form a paste and season to taste with salt and pepper. Rub the entire outside of the chicken with the herb paste. Place the chicken, breast side up, on a rack in a roasting pan. Roast until an instant-read thermometer inserted into the thickest part of the breast away from the bone registers 170°F (77°C), or until the juices run clear when a thigh is pierced with a knife, about 1 hour and 40 minutes. Slip the extra stuffing into the oven during the last 20 minutes of cooking.

Remove the chicken from the oven and transfer to a platter. Cover loosely with aluminum foil and let stand for 5–10 minutes. Remove the baking dish of stuffing and keep warm. Spoon the stuffing from the cavity into the baking dish. Carve the chicken and serve with the stuffing.

Serves 4–6

1 lb (500 g) spinach

2 tablespoons unsalted butter

1 yellow onion, chopped

1 cup (3 oz/90 g) sliced fresh cremini mushrooms

2 cloves garlic, chopped

2 teaspoons *each* chopped fresh tarragon, flat-leaf (Italian) parsley, and marjoram

2 cups (10 oz/315 g) cooked white rice

1 cup (8 oz/250 g) ricotta cheese

1 egg, beaten

Salt and freshly ground pepper

1/3 cup (1 1/2 oz/45 g) pine nuts, toasted

1 chicken, 3 1/2–4 lb (1.75–2 kg)

FOR THE HERB PASTE:

2 tablespoons olive oil

2 cloves garlic, minced

2 teaspoons paprika

2 teaspoons *each* minced fresh tarragon and flat-leaf (Italian) parsley

Salt and freshly ground pepper

Roast Chicken with Garlic and Herbs

Preheat the oven to 425°F (220°C). Rinse the chicken and pat dry with paper towels.

In a small bowl, combine the garlic, paprika, marjoram, basil, chervil, rosemary, and olive oil. Mix well to form a paste and season to taste with salt and pepper. Using your fingers and beginning at the neck opening, gently loosen the skin on the chicken breasts, thighs, and legs; be careful not to tear the skin. Rub about three-fourths of the paste under the skin evenly over the breast, thigh, and leg meat. Gently pat the skin in place and then rub the skin of the entire bird with the remaining one fourth of the paste. Using kitchen string, tie the drumsticks together. Tuck the wing tips under the body. Place the chicken, breast side up, on a rack in a roasting pan.

Place in the oven and reduce the heat to 350°F (180°C). Roast until an instant-read thermometer inserted into the thickest part of the breast registers 170°F (77°C) or until the juices run clear when a thigh is pierced with a knife, about $1^{1}/_{4}$ hours. Remove from the oven and transfer to a platter. Cover loosely with aluminum foil and let stand for 5–10 minutes before carving.

Meanwhile, pour the pan drippings from the roasting pan into a small saucepan. Skim the fat off the top. Place the roasting pan on the stove top over high heat. Add the stock and wine and deglaze the pan, stirring to remove any browned bits from the pan bottom. Remove from the heat. Place the saucepan holding the drippings over medium heat and add the flour. Cook, stirring, until beginning to brown, about $1^{1}/_{2}$ minutes. Add the stock from the roasting pan, bring to a boil, and cook until reduced to the desired consistency, 5–10 minutes. Season with salt and pepper and pour into a warmed sauceboat.

Carve the chicken and serve. Pass the gravy at the table.

Serves 4

1 chicken, $3^{1}/_{2}$–4 lb (1.75–2 kg)

3 cloves garlic, minced

1 tablespoon paprika

2 teaspoons minced fresh marjoram

2 teaspoons minced fresh basil

2 teaspoons minced fresh chervil

2 teaspoons minced fresh rosemary

2 tablespoons pure olive oil

Salt and freshly ground pepper

$^{3}/_{4}$ cup (6 fl oz/180 ml) Chicken Stock (page 288) or broth

$^{1}/_{4}$ cup (2 fl oz/60 ml) dry white wine

$1^{1}/_{2}$ tablespoons all-purpose (plain) flour

Harvesttime Chicken and Peppers

6 tablespoons (2¼ oz/67 g) all-purpose (plain) flour

4 chicken breast halves, about ½ lb (250 g) each, skinned

4 chicken thighs, about 6 oz (185 g) each, skinned

4 chicken drumsticks, about ¼ lb (125 g) each, skinned

2 tablespoons olive oil

Salt and freshly ground pepper

1 yellow onion, halved and sliced

½ red bell pepper (capsicum), seeded and sliced crosswise

½ green bell pepper (capsicum), seeded and sliced crosswise

½ yellow bell pepper (capsicum), seeded and sliced crosswise

2 cloves garlic, minced

1 tablespoon minced fresh basil

1 tablespoon minced fresh oregano

1 tablespoon minced fresh flat-leaf (Italian) parsley

3 cups (18 oz/560 g) peeled, seeded, and chopped tomatoes

1 cup (8 fl oz/250 ml) Chicken Stock (page 288) or broth

½ cup (4 fl oz/125 ml) dry white wine

Preheat the oven to 350°F (180°C).

Spread the flour on a plate, then lightly coat both sides of each chicken piece with the flour, shaking off the excess.

In a frying pan over high heat, warm the olive oil. Add the chicken in batches and sauté, turning once, until lightly browned, about 2 minutes on each side. Transfer to a baking dish large enough to hold all the chicken in a single layer. Repeat until all the chicken is browned, then season with salt and pepper and set aside.

Reduce the heat to medium and add the onion, bell peppers, garlic, basil, oregano, and parsley. Sauté until softened, about 5 minutes. Stir in the tomatoes, stock, and wine, raise the heat to high, and bring to a boil. Pour the mixture evenly over the chicken.

Cover and bake until the chicken is opaque throughout and the juices run clear when a thigh is pierced with a knife, 20–30 minutes.

Uncover and serve hot, directly from the dish.

Serves 6

Grilled Chicken Breasts with Tarragon Mustard

A tangy tarragon-mustard marinade complements this simple grilled chicken dish. Cooking the whole breast makes an attractive presentation for company. Carve the meat from the bone into thick slices so that each slice has a grill-marked edge.

In a small bowl, whisk together the wine, mustard, oil, garlic, 2 teaspoons of the tarragon, the sugar, salt, and pepper. Scoop out and reserve $^{1}/_{4}$ cup (2 fl oz/60 ml) of the mustard mixture. Place the chicken in a nonaluminum dish. Pour the remaining mustard mixture evenly over the top, cover with plastic wrap, and refrigerate, turning the chicken occasionally, for at least 1 hour or for up to 4 hours.

Prepare a hot fire for indirect-heat cooking in a covered grill (see pages 8–9). Position the grill rack 4–6 inches (10–15 cm) above the fire.

About 20 minutes before the fire is ready, remove the chicken from the refrigerator and bring it to room temperature. When the fire is hot, place the chicken on the perimeter of the grill rack directly over the fire. Grill, turning once, until seared on both sides with grill marks, about 2 minutes on each side. Move the chicken pieces, bone side down, to the center of the grill rack so they are not directly over the fire. Cover the grill, open the vents halfway, and cook, turning once or twice and basting occasionally with the reserved marinade, until the chicken is opaque throughout and the juices run clear when the meat is pierced with a knife, about 20 minutes.

Transfer to a warmed serving platter, carve into slices, and sprinkle with the remaining 1 teaspoon tarragon; serve immediately.

Serves 4

1/3 cup (3 fl oz/80 ml) dry white wine

2–3 tablespoons tarragon-flavored mustard

2 tablespoons extra-virgin olive oil

2 cloves garlic, minced

3 teaspoons finely chopped fresh tarragon

1 teaspoon sugar

1/4 teaspoon salt

1/4 teaspoon freshly ground pepper

2 whole chicken breasts, about 1 lb (500 g) each, skinned

Cornish Hens au Poivre

The unusual spice mixture used on these elegant little birds has a unique peppery base. The mixture penetrates through the skin during the dry marinating time and then seasons the hens more completely during roasting.

FOR THE SPICED PEPPERCORNS:

3 tablespoons mixed peppercorns

1/4 teaspoon red pepper flakes

8 whole allspice

8 juniper berries

6 Cornish hens, 1–1¼ lb (1–1.25 kg) each

1 tablespoon coarse salt

3–4 tablespoons olive oil

Juice of 2 lemons

Watercress sprigs

In a bowl, stir together the peppercorns, red pepper flakes, allspice, and juniper berries. Transfer to a pepper mill or spice grinder and grind coarsely. Set aside.

One hour before roasting, rinse the hens and pat dry with paper towels. Using a sharp knife or kitchen shears, split each hen in half down the back and the breastbone. Tuck the leg into the skin, pushing it up to meet the breastbone, and fold back the wing of each hen half. Using the flat side of a cleaver, pound the skin side of each half to flatten the meat and facilitate even cooking. In a small bowl, combine the spiced peppercorns and the salt, and generously rub the surface of the hen halves with the mixture. Place the hen halves, skin sides up, in a shallow roasting pan large enough to hold them in a single layer. Let stand, uncovered, for 1 hour at room temperature.

Preheat the oven to 425°F (220°C). Arrange the hen halves, skin sides down, in the pan. Drizzle 1/4 teaspoon of the olive oil and 1/4 teaspoon of the lemon juice over each half. Roast until the meat begins to brown, about 12 minutes. Turn over the birds and baste with the remaining oil and lemon juice. Continue to roast until the skin is crisp and browned or until an instant-read thermometer inserted into the thickest part of the breast, away from the bone, registers 165°–170°F (74°–77°C), 25–30 minutes longer. Transfer the hens to a warmed platter and let rest for 5–10 minutes before serving.

While the hens are resting, spoon off the fat from the pan juices. Strain the pan juices through a fine-mesh sieve into a warmed bowl and keep warm.

Garnish the hens with watercress and serve. Pass the pan juices at the table.

Serves 6

Grilled Chicken, Korean Style

Seasonings typical of Korean cooking—soy sauce, garlic, ginger, toasted sesame seeds, and green onions—flavor this grilled chicken, called *dak bulgogi*. Serve with steamed rice and stir-fried spinach or other leafy greens.

Place each chicken piece between 2 sheets of plastic wrap. Using a meat pounder, gently pound the meat to uniform thickness of $1/4$ inch (6 mm). Place in a glass bowl and coat evenly with the lemon juice.

In a small, dry frying pan over low heat, toast the sesame seeds, stirring occasionally, until fragrant and golden brown, 3–5 minutes. Set aside 1 tablespoon of the toasted seeds. Transfer the remaining 1 tablespoon seeds to a spice grinder and grind to a powder, or transfer to a mortar and grind with a pestle.

In a small bowl, stir together the ground sesame seeds, garlic, minced green onions, soy sauces, sugar, sesame oil, ginger, and pepper. Pour the mixture over the chicken, turn the pieces to coat evenly, cover, and refrigerate for at least 3 hours or as long as overnight.

Prepare a hot fire for direct-heat cooking in a grill (see pages 8–9). Position the grill rack 4–6 inches (10–15 cm) above the fire.

Place the chicken pieces directly on the grill rack. Grill until lightly charred, about 5 minutes. Turn and cook until charred on the second side, 3–4 minutes longer. Transfer to a serving platter.

Sprinkle the chicken with the reserved sesame seeds and the slivered green onions and serve immediately.

Serves 6

$1^1/_2$ lb (750 g) skinless, boneless chicken breasts, thighs, or a combination

2 tablespoons lemon juice

2 tablespoons sesame seeds

2 cloves garlic, minced

2 green (spring) onions, including the tender green tops, minced, plus 3 green onions, white parts only, cut into fine slivers

$1/4$ cup (2 fl oz/60 ml) light soy sauce

$1/4$ cup (2 fl oz/60 ml) dark soy sauce

2 tablespoons sugar

$1^1/_2$ tablespoons Asian sesame oil

2 teaspoons peeled and minced fresh ginger

$1/2$ teaspoon freshly ground pepper

Spicy Grilled Chicken with Kaffir Lime

3 small chickens, about 2 lb (1 kg) each, quartered

1 tablespoon lime juice

3 teaspoons salt

4 candlenuts or blanched almonds

8 red jalapeño chiles, seeded and quartered

6 cloves garlic, sliced

5 stalks lemongrass, center white part only, chopped

5 shallots or 1 small yellow onion, quartered

1 piece fresh ginger, about 3/4 inch (2 cm)

1 teaspoon ground turmeric

1 can (13 1/2 fl oz/425 ml) unsweetened coconut milk, shaken well

1/4 cup (2 fl oz/60 ml) peanut or corn oil

2 tablespoons sugar

10 fresh or frozen kaffir lime leaves, center spines removed leaves very finely shredded

2 limes, cut lengthwise into wedges

6 sprigs fresh cilantro (fresh coriander)

Using a fork, pierce the chicken quarters all over. Place in a glass bowl, coat with the lime juice and 1 teaspoon of the salt, and set aside.

Place the nuts in a small bowl, add water to cover, and soak until moist, about 10 minutes. Drain. In a blender, combine the nuts, jalapeños, garlic, lemongrass, shallots, ginger, turmeric, and just enough water to facilitate blending, 2–4 tablespoons. Process until a smooth paste forms. Transfer to a large bowl and add the coconut milk. You should have about 3 cups (24 fl oz/750 ml) liquid. Add 1/2 cup (4 fl oz/125 ml) of the mixture to the chicken, coat evenly, cover, and refrigerate for at least 1 hour or up to overnight. Refrigerate the remaining liquid.

Warm a large saucepan or wok over medium heat. Add the oil and the remaining coconut milk mixture and cook, stirring frequently, until emulsified and fragrant, about 3 minutes. Continue to cook until beads of oil appear in the mixture, about 8 minutes. Add the sugar, the remaining 2 teaspoons salt, and three-fourths of the shredded lime leaves. Reduce the heat to low and simmer until the sugar is dissolved, about 1 minute. Taste and adjust the seasonings. Set the sauce aside.

Prepare a hot fire for direct-heat cooking in a grill (see pages 8–9). Position grill rack 4–6 inches (10–15 cm) above the fire.

Place the chicken, skin side down, directly on the grill rack and grill until golden brown, about 15 minutes. Turn and cook until golden brown, about 15 minutes. An instant-read thermometer inserted into the thickest part of the breast away from the bone should register 170°F (77°C); in the thigh, it should register 185°F (85°C). Transfer the chicken to a serving dish, sprinkle with the remaining 1/4 lime leaves and garnish with the lime wedges and coriander sprigs. Serve hot, passing the reserved sauce at the table.

Serves 6

Cornish Hens with Grapes and Sage

Cornish hens are perfect to serve to company. In this recipe, the dark grapes and sage in the stuffing suggest pouring a light-to medium-bodied red wine. Serve with a simple risotto or a mixed green salad.

Rinse the birds and pat dry with paper towels. Generously sprinkle inside and out with salt and pepper.

Using your fingers, carefully loosen the breast skin on each bird. Tuck 4 sage leaves evenly under the skin and over the breast of each Cornish hen. Pat the skin firmly back in place. Tuck 2 sage leaves inside the cavity of each bird.

Preheat the oven to 350°F (180°C).

In a large sauté pan over medium-high heat, melt the butter with the olive oil. Add the birds and cook, turning often, until well browned on all sides, 10–15 minutes. Transfer the birds to a roasting pan and place in the oven. Roast until the juices run clear when a leg is pierced with a knife, 35–45 minutes.

While the birds are roasting, in a blender or food processor, process the 2 cups (12 oz/375 g) grapes until puréed. Pour the chicken stock into a small saucepan and place over high heat. Bring to a boil and boil until reduced by half, 8–10 minutes. Add the puréed grapes and chopped sage, reduce the heat to medium, and simmer until slightly thickened, about 5 minutes. Add the halved grapes and heat until warmed through.

Transfer the birds to warmed individual plates. If desired, cut the Cornish hens in half with poultry shears. Spoon the sauce over the birds and serve immediately.

Serves 4

4 Cornish hens, about 1 lb (500 g) each

Salt and freshly ground pepper

24 fresh sage leaves, plus 2 tablespoons chopped fresh sage

2 tablespoons unsalted butter

2 tablespoons olive oil

2 cups (12 oz/375 g) red or black seedless grapes, plus 1 cup (6 oz/185 g) grapes, halved

1 cup (8 fl oz/250 ml) Chicken Stock (page 288), or broth

Grilled Duck with Red Curry Sauce

Roasted Chinese duck—as seen hanging in storefront windows—is traditionally used for this Thai recipe. When roasted duck is not available, it is easy to marinate and grill your own, as directed below. Steamed rice makes a good accompaniment.

1 clove garlic, minced

1 tablespoon granulated sugar

1 tablespoon rice wine

2 teaspoons light soy sauce

1¹/₂ teaspoons Asian sesame oil

1 teaspoon dark soy sauce

1 teaspoon peeled and minced fresh ginger

¹/₂ teaspoon five-spice powder

¹/₂ teaspoon salt, plus salt to taste

6 duck breast halves, about 4–6 oz (125–185 g) each

2 cans (13¹/₂ fl oz/425 ml each) unsweetened coconut milk

2 tablespoons Thai red curry paste

1 tablespoons Thai fish sauce

1 tablespoon dark brown sugar

8 kaffir lime leaves

4 red chiles, seeded and sliced

1 cup (6 oz/185 g) diced fresh pineapple

¹/₂ cup (¹/₂ oz/15 g) fresh basil, plus leaves for garnish

Freshly ground pepper

In a large glass bowl, combine the garlic, granulated sugar, rice wine, light soy sauce, sesame oil, dark soy sauce, ginger, five-spice powder, and ¹/₄ teaspoon salt. Using a fork, prick the duck skin at 1-inch (2.5-cm) intervals. Add the duck to the bowl and turn to coat evenly, rubbing the marinade on both sides of the breast halves. Cover and refrigerate for 4 hours or up to overnight.

Prepare a medium-hot fire for direct-heat cooking in a charcoal grill (see pages 8–9). Position the grill rack 4–6 inches (10–15 cm) above the fire. Meanwhile, carefully open the cans of coconut milk. Spoon the thick layer of cream on top into a bowl. In a saucepan over medium-high heat, combine ¹/₂ cup (4 fl oz/125 ml) of the coconut cream and the red curry paste and cook, stirring frequently, until the cream is aromatic and beads of oil float on top, about 3 minutes. Add the fish sauce, brown sugar, lime leaves, chiles, and remaining coconut milk. Cook, stirring occasionally, until heated through, about 5 minutes. Stir in the pineapple and the ¹/₂ cup (¹/₂ oz/ 15 g) basil. Remove from the heat and keep warm while grilling the duck.

Remove the duck from the marinade, discarding the marinade, and place skin side down on the grill rack. Grill until the fat is rendered and the skin is crisp, about 8 minutes. Turn and grill until the duck is fully cooked and feels firm to the touch on the second side, 3–5 minutes. Season to taste with salt and pepper.

Slice the duck across the grain ¹/₄ inch (6 mm) thick slices. Arrange 1 sliced duck breast half on each plate. Spoon the curry sauce over the top, garnish with the basil leaves, and serve.

Serves 6

Malaysian-Style Chicken with Satay Sauce

Serve this classic Southeast Asian dish as part of an array of regional small plates. Look for canned coconut milk in the Asian or ethnic foods section of your market. If the sauce becomes too thick, thin it with a little hot water.

In a nonaluminum bowl, combine 1 cup (8 fl oz/250 ml) of the coconut milk and the ginger. Add the chicken pieces and turn to coat evenly. Cover and refrigerate for 2 hours. Remove from the refrigerator 30 minutes before grilling. At the same time, put 8 bamboo skewers in water to cover for at least 30 minutes.

To make the satay sauce, in a small bowl, combine the chiles and hot water. Let stand for about 20 minutes. Meanwhile, in a small frying pan over medium-low heat, warm the peanut oil. Add the onion and sauté for about 1 minute. Add the garlic and sauté until fragrant, about 2 minutes. Add the soy sauce and turmeric and sauté until the onion is soft, 4–5 minutes longer. Remove from the heat and let cool.

In a food processor, grind the peanuts coarsely; do not process to a paste. Transfer to a bowl and set aside. Add the soaked chiles, 3 tablespoons of the soaking liquid, and the onion-garlic mixture to the food processor and process until smooth. Add the remaining 1 cup (8 fl oz/250 ml) coconut milk, the ground nuts, and the lemon juice and process just until mixed. Transfer to a heatproof bowl. Place over (not touching) barely simmering water and cook, stirring occasionally, until hot, about 15 minutes. Keep warm until ready to serve.

Prepare a hot fire for direct-heat cooking in a grill (see pages 8–9). Position the grill rack 4–6 inches (10–15 cm) above the fire. Thread the chicken pieces onto the skewers, and place the skewers on the rack. Grill, turning once, until the chicken is opaque throughout and the juices run clear when the meat is pierced with a knife, 4–5 minutes on each side. Transfer to a platter and serve hot. Pass the sauce at the table.

Serves 4

1 can (14 fl oz/440 ml) light coconut milk

1 teaspoon peeled and minced fresh ginger

2 whole skinless, boneless, chicken breasts, about 1½ lb (750 g) total weight, cut into 1-inch (2.5-cm) pieces

FOR THE SATAY SAUCE:

2 small dried chiles, seeded and chopped

¼ cup (2 fl oz/60 ml) hot water

2 tablespoons peanut oil

1 small yellow onion, chopped

1 clove garlic, chopped

1 tablespoon soy sauce

1 teaspoon ground turmeric

1 cup (5 oz/155 g) dry-roasted peanuts

1 tablespoon lemon juice

Grilled Chicken in a North African Marinade

Serve with a wine such as a spicy Gewurztraminer, which will subtly bring out the exotic character of the aromatics (anise, saffron, ginger, and cinnamon) in this spicy grilled chicken. Serve with couscous, a lemon wedge, and assorted grilled vegetables.

2 tablespoons aniseed

¼ cup (⅓ oz/10 g) chopped fresh cilantro (fresh coriander)

¼ cup (¾ oz/20 g) chopped green (spring) onion, including the tender green tops

4 cloves garlic, chopped

2 teaspoons paprika

2 teaspoons ground coriander

1 teaspoon ground ginger

1 teaspoon ground cinnamon

½ teaspoon saffron threads, finely chopped

½ teaspoon cayenne pepper

¼ cup (2 fl oz/60 ml) lemon juice

2 tablespoons honey

½ cup (4 fl oz/125 ml) olive oil, or as needed

Freshly ground black pepper

2 broiler chickens, each about 2½ lb (1.25 kg), split

Salt

In a small sauté pan over medium heat, toast the aniseed, shaking the pan often, until fragrant, 3–4 minutes. Remove from the heat, let cool slightly, and transfer to a mortar. Grind the toasted seeds coarsely with a pestle and transfer to a food processor. Add the cilantro, green onion, garlic, paprika, coriander, ginger, cinnamon, saffron, and cayenne pepper. Using on-off pulses, pulse to combine. Add the lemon juice and honey and again pulse to combine. The mixture should be pasty. Transfer to a bowl and whisk in ½ cup (4 fl oz/125 ml) olive oil until well incorporated, adding more as needed to create a smooth mixture. Season with generous grindings of black pepper. The marinade should be good and spicy.

Rinse the chickens and pat dry with paper towels. Place in a nonaluminum container and coat evenly with the marinade. Cover and refrigerate overnight. Bring the chicken to room temperature before grilling.

Prepare a hot fire for direct-heat cooking in a charcoal grill (see pages 8–9). Position the grill rack 4–6 inches (10–15 cm) above the fire.

Season the chicken with salt and place, skin side up, on the oiled grill rack. Grill until well browned, about 6 minutes. Turn and continue to grill until the skin is well browned and caramelized and the meat is cooked through, 5–6 minutes longer. The juices should run clear when a leg is pierced with a knife.

Transfer to a warmed platter or individual plates and serve immediately.

Serves 4

Cornish Hens with Olive Oil and Rosemary

A good-quality extra-virgin olive oil is a must for this recipe, as the hens take on its flavor as they marinate. Polenta, topped with Ratatouille on the Grill (page 266), makes the perfect accompaniment.

Place each hen, breast side down, on a work surface. With heavy-duty kitchen scissors, cut from the neck to the tail along both sides of the backbone; discard the backbone. Trim any excess fat, turn breast side up, tuck in the wings, and press down firmly on the breastbone to flatten the bird.

Pour $1/2$ cup (4 fl oz/125 ml) of the olive oil into 2 nonaluminum dishes large enough to hold the hens flat, dividing the oil evenly. Place the hens in the oil, skin sides down. Pour the remaining $1/2$ cup (4 fl oz/125 ml) oil over the hens, making sure they are entirely coated. Use a brush, if necessary, to coat evenly. Cover with plastic wrap and place a heavy weight on top of each hen. Refrigerate for 36 hours.

In a small bowl, stir together the black pepper, salt, rosemary, and cayenne pepper. Remove the hens from the oil and sprinkle the pepper mixture evenly over both sides of each hen. Rub the mixture into the hens and then sprinkle them with the lemon juice. Cover and let stand at room temperature for 1 hour.

Prepare a hot fire for direct-heat cooking in a covered grill (see pages 8–9). Position the grill rack 4–6 inches (10–15 cm) above the fire. Place the hens, skin sides down, on the rack. Cover the grill and open the vents. Cook until the undersides are browned and crisp, about 15 minutes. (If the skin is not crisp enough at this point, remove the cover briefly.) Turn over the hens, cover, and continue to cook until they are nicely browned on the second sides and the juices run clear when a thigh is pierced with a knife at the thickest point, about 15 minutes longer. Transfer the hens to individual plates and serve.

Serves 4

4 Cornish hens, 1–1¼ lb (500–625 g) each

1 cup (8 fl oz/250 ml) extra-virgin olive oil

2 teaspoons coarsely ground black pepper

1 teaspoon coarse salt

1 teaspoon chopped fresh rosemary or ½ teaspoon dried rosemary

½ teaspoon cayenne pepper

¼ cup (2 fl oz/60 ml) lemon juice

Spicy Chicken, Saint Lucian Style

Whether dining al fresco on the West Indian island of Saint Lucia or under a maple tree in your own backyard, you'll find this spicy dish refreshing. Flavorful, with just a touch of sweetness, the chicken is beautifully complemented by a fresh fruit salsa.

3 tablespoons dark brown sugar

2 tablespoons chopped fresh parsley

1 tablespoon chopped fresh cilantro (fresh coriander)

1/2 teaspoon chopped fresh thyme

1/2 teaspoon ground cumin

1/2 teaspoon ground turmeric

1/2 teaspoon curry powder

4 teaspoons olive oil

1 large clove garlic, minced

1 yellow onion, halved and sliced

2 chickens, about 3 lb (1.5 kg) each, cut into serving pieces

In a bowl, combine the brown sugar and $1/3$ cup (3 fl oz/80 ml) hot water and stir until the sugar dissolves. Add the parsley, cilantro, thyme, cumin, turmeric, curry powder, olive oil, garlic, and onion and mix well to form a marinade.

Place the chicken pieces in a shallow nonaluminum dish. Spoon the marinade over the chicken, turning to coat evenly. Cover and refrigerate for 24 hours, turning the chicken several times. Remove from the refrigerator 30 minutes before grilling.

Prepare a hot fire for direct-heat cooking in a covered grill (see pages 8–9). Position the grill rack 4–6 inches (10–15 cm) above the fire.

Place the drumsticks and thighs on the center of the rack. Cover the grill and open the vents halfway. Cook, turning once, until browned, about 7 minutes on each side. Move the drumsticks and thighs to the outer edges of the rack and place the breasts and wings in the center of the skin. Cover and cook until browned, about 8 minutes. Turn over all the chicken pieces and continue to cook until the skin is crisp and the juices run clear when a thigh is pierced with a knife at the thickest part, about 8 minutes longer. Serve immediately.

Serves 6

Deviled Turkey Burgers

Turkey burgers, when properly prepared, are just as juicy and tasty as beef burgers, especially when cooked on a grill. Try these topped with a slice of your favorite cheese and serve with corn on the cob, coleslaw, and potato salad.

In a bowl, combine the turkey, green onions, mustard, egg white, salt, and pepper. Mix well and shape into 4 patties each about 3/4 inch (1.5 cm) thick.

Prepare a hot fire for direct-heat cooking in a grill (see pages 8–9). Position the grill rack 4–6 inches (10–15 cm) above the fire.

Place the patties on the rack. Cook, turning once, until firm to the touch, about 6 minutes on each side. Just before the patties are done, place the buns or rolls, cut sides down, around the edges of the rack and toast lightly.

Transfer the buns or rolls, cut sides up, to individual plates and top the bottom half of each with a lettuce leaf, a tomato slice, and then a patty. Replace the top halves of the bun. Serve immediately.

Serves 4

1 1/3 lb (655 g) ground (minced) turkey

2 small green (spring) onions, finely chopped

2 teaspoons Dijon mustard

1 egg white, lightly beaten

1/4 teaspoon salt

1/4 teaspoon freshly ground pepper

4 hamburger buns or rolls, split lengthwise

4 lettuce leaves

4 large tomato slices

Turkey-Stuffed Peppers

These Italian-influenced peppers are best served hot off the grill, drizzled with olive oil and vinegar. For a spicier dish, use half hot and half sweet sausages. When selecting peppers, choose short, squat peppers that stand up on their own.

6 green bell peppers (capsicums)

10 oz (315 g) Italian-style turkey sausage, casings removed

1 yellow onion, finely chopped

1 clove garlic, minced

1 tablespoon curry powder

1/2 teaspoon freshly ground pepper

1/4 teaspoon salt

2 eggs, lightly beaten

1/3 cup (3 fl oz/80 ml) Chicken Stock (page 288) or broth

1 1/2 cups (7 oz/235 g) cooked white rice

3 tablespoons fine dried bread crumbs

2 tablespoons grated Parmesan cheese

1 tablespoon olive oil

Cut a slice off the top of each pepper and remove the seeds. Bring a large saucepan three-fourths full of water to a boil. Add the bell peppers and blanch for 1 minute. Drain well and set aside.

In a frying pan over medium heat, cook the sausage, breaking up the lumps with a wooden spoon, until the meat begins to lose its pink color, about 5 minutes. Add the onion, garlic, curry powder, pepper, and salt and cook, stirring frequently, until the onion is soft, about 10 minutes. Transfer to a bowl and let cool slightly.

Add the eggs to the sausage mixture and mix well. Stir in the chicken broth and rice and again mix well.

Spoon the sausage mixture into the peppers, dividing it evenly. Sprinkle the tops with the bread crumbs, Parmesan, and olive oil, again dividing evenly.

Prepare a hot fire for direct-heat cooking in a covered grill (see pages 8–9). Position the grill rack 4–6 inches (10–15 cm) above the fire.

Place the peppers on the grill rack. Cover the grill and open the vents halfway. Cook until the peppers are tender when pierced with a knife, about 40 minutes. If the peppers start to burn on the bottom, move them to the outer edges of the rack.

Transfer the peppers to individual plates and serve hot.

Serves 6

Tandoori Chicken with Toasted Pappadams

Pat the chicken pieces dry with paper towels. Make deep diagonal slashes almost to the bone at 1½-inch (4-cm) intervals across the meaty side of each piece. Place in a glass bowl and rub with the lime juice. Cover and refrigerate for 30 minutes.

Meanwhile, prepare the marinade: In a small, dry frying pan over low heat, toast the coriander and cumin seeds, stirring occasionally, until fragrant, about 3 minutes. Transfer to a spice grinder and grind to a powder, or transfer to a mortar and grind to a powder with a pestle. In a blender, combine the garlic, ginger, salt, and enough water to facilitate blending (1–2 tablespoons). Process until a smooth paste forms. Add the toasted cumin and coriander seeds, paprika, turmeric, cayenne, yogurt, and lime juice and purée until smooth. Pour into a large lock-top plastic bag, add the chicken pieces, seal, and turn the bag to coat the pieces evenly. Refrigerate for at least 4 hours or as long as overnight. Bring the chicken to room temperature before grilling.

Preheat a broiler (grill). If using the pappadams, place a cake rack over a gas or electric burner. Working with 1 pappadam at a time, place on the rack over medium-high heat. Using tongs, rotate the water continuously until completely opaque and covered with tiny bubbles and brown flecks, about 30 seconds. Turn and toast until crisp, about 30 seconds longer.

Place the chicken, slashed sides up, on the broiler pan and brush with the oil. Broil (grill) 2–3 inches (5–7.5 cm) from the heat source until browned, about 20 minutes. Turn, brush with oil, and grill until browned on the second side, about 10 minutes longer.

Transfer to a serving platter and top with the onion and cucumber. Sprinkle with cilantro and mint and garnish with lime wedges. Serve with the toasted pappadams, if using.

Serves 6–8

3 lb (1.5 kg) skinless chicken thighs or breasts

3 tablespoons lime juice

FOR THE MARINADE:

1 tablespoon coriander seeds

1 teaspoon cumin seeds

4 cloves garlic

1 piece fresh ginger, about 1 inch (2.5 cm), peeled

1 teaspoon salt

1 teaspoon paprika

½ teaspoon ground turmeric

½ teaspoon cayenne pepper

½ cup (4 oz/125 g) plain yogurt

1 tablespoon lime juice

8 pappadam wafers (optional)

Vegetable oil for brushing

1 white onion, thinly sliced

1 small English (hothouse) cucumber, peeled and thinly sliced

3 tablespoons coarsely chopped fresh cilantro (fresh coriander)

2 tablespoons coarsely chopped fresh mint

2 limes, cut lengthwise into wedges

Chicken Teriyaki

Chicken takes on a beautiful mahogany finish when brushed with this Japanese-style glaze. The saltiness imparted by the soy sauce complements the smoky flavor from the fire. Using both mirin (sweet rice wine) and dry sake adds depth to the sauce.

½ cup (4 fl oz/125 ml) soy sauce

¼ cup (2 fl oz/60 ml) mirin

¼ cup (2 fl oz/60 ml) dry sake or dry sherry

1 tablespoon peeled and chopped fresh ginger

2 cloves garlic, minced

1 teaspoon brown sugar

4 skinless, boneless chicken breast halves, about 6 oz (185 g) each

Prepare a hot fire for direct-heat cooking in a grill (see pages 8–9). Position the grill rack 4–6 inches (10–15 cm) above the fire.

In a small saucepan over high heat, combine the soy sauce, mirin, sake, ginger, garlic, and brown sugar. Stir well and bring to a boil. Boil for 1 minute, then remove from the heat, pour into a shallow bowl, and let cool completely.

One at a time, place the chicken breasts between 2 sheets of plastic wrap. Use a meat pounder to flatten to an even ½ inch (12 mm) thick. Cover and refrigerate until needed.

About 15 minutes before the fire is ready, scoop out and reserve about ½ cup (4 fl oz/125 ml) of the soy mixture to use for basting. Then, place the chicken breasts in the remaining cooled soy mixture.

When the fire is hot, remove the chicken from the soy mixture and place on the grill rack directly over the fire. Discard any soy mixture remaining in the bowl. Grill, turning once and brushing with some of the reserved soy mixture, until the chicken is opaque throughout and the juices run clear when meat is pierced with a knife, about 4 minutes on each side.

Transfer the chicken to a serving platter, brush with the remaining reserved soy mixture, and serve.

Serves 4

Classic Barbecued Chicken

In a small heatproof bowl, combine the ancho chile and boiling water. Let stand until the chile has softened, about 20 minutes. Drain, reserving $^1/_4$ cup (2 fl oz/60 ml) of the liquid. In a food processor, combine the softened chile, the reserved liquid, and the olive oil. Process until a thick, smooth paste forms. Rub the chicken pieces with the paste and place in a shallow nonaluminum dish. Cover and refrigerate for at least 2 hours or for up to 24 hours. Remove from the refrigerator 30 minutes before grilling.

Meanwhile, make the sauce: In a saucepan over medium-low heat, melt the butter. Add the onion and cook until softened, about 5 minutes. Stir in the ketchup, $^1/_2$ cup (4 fl oz/125 ml) water, the Worcestershire sauce, steak sauce, vinegar, and brown sugar. Bring to a boil, reduce the heat to low, cover partially, and simmer until thickened slightly, about 20 minutes. Set aside.

Prepare a hot fire for direct-heat cooking in a covered grill (see pages 8–9). Position the grill rack 4–6 inches (10–15 cm) above the fire. Place the drumsticks and thighs on the center of the rack and cover the grill. Cook, turning once, until browned, about 7 minutes on each side. Move the drumsticks and thighs to the outer edges of the rack and place the breasts and wings in the center. Cover and cook until browned, about 8 minutes. Turn over all the pieces and continue to cook until the juices run clear when a thigh is pierced with a knife, about 8 minutes longer.

Meanwhile, reheat the barbecue sauce. Transfer $^1/_2$ cup (4 fl oz/120 ml) of the sauce to a small heatproof bowl.

Brush the chicken with $^1/_4$ cup (2 fl oz/60 ml) of the reserved barbecue sauce. Turn over the chicken and brush with the remaining $^1/_4$ cup (2 fl oz/ 60 ml) sauce. Cook uncovered, turning once, until crisp, about 2 minutes on each side.

Transfer to a platter and serve. Pass the remaining sauce at the table.

Serves 6

1 ancho chile, seeded and cut into pieces

1 cup (8 fl oz/250 ml) boiling water

1 tablespoon olive oil

2 chickens, about 3$^1/_2$ lb (1.75 kg) each, cut into serving pieces

FOR THE BARBECUE SAUCE:

2 tablespoons unsalted butter

1 yellow onion, finely chopped

1$^1/_2$ cups (12 fl oz/375 ml) tomato ketchup

$^1/_3$ cup (3 fl oz/80 ml) Worcestershire sauce

$^1/_4$ cup (2 fl oz/60 ml) steak sauce

2 tablespoons cider vinegar

$^1/_3$ cup (2$^1/_2$ oz/75 g) firmly packed brown sugar

Beef & Lamb

Hamburger on Garlic Toast with Watercress and Stilton

Here's an elegant burger, served open-faced with crisp garlic toast and watercress on the bottom and crumbled Stilton on top. Use extra watercress to make a salad, adding some Belgian endive (chicory/witloof) and a mustard vinaigrette, if you like.

1 lb (500 g) ground (minced) beef chuck

1$^1/_2$ teaspoons salt

Freshly ground pepper

$^1/_4$ cup finely minced green (spring) onion, white and pale green parts only

3 tablespoons olive oil

4 oz (125 g) Stilton cheese, at room temperature

4 slices coarse country bread, about $^1/_3$ inch (9 mm) thick

2 cloves garlic, halved

2 cups (2 oz/60 g) watercress leaves, thick stems removed

Place the beef in a bowl and season with the salt and pepper to taste. Stir in the onion, mixing well. Gently shape into 4 patties, each $^1/_2$ inch (12 mm) thick.

Prepare a hot fire for direct-heat cooking on a grill (see pages 8–9). Place the patties on the hottest part of the grill and cover the grill. Grill until the underside is crisp, 4–5 minutes. Turn over the patties, and grill until done to your liking, about 4 minutes for medium.

While the hamburgers cooks on the second side, crumble half of the Stilton on top. Using a knife, smash the Stilton so that it melts onto the hamburgers. Transfer the hamburgers to a plate; keep warm.

Place the bread slices around the edges of the grill rack and toast lightly. Remove from the grill and rub one side well with the cut sides of the halved garlic clove. Put 1 piece of toast on each of 4 individual plates, garlic-rubbed side up. Top with the remaining Stilton, crumbling it evenly over the toast, then with the watercress. Top the watercress with a patty. Serve hot.

Serves 4

Eye of Round with Vegetables

In a large nonaluminum bowl, combine the wine, Cognac, chopped garlic and onion, bay leaf, and rosemary. Tie the peppercorns and cloves in a piece of cheesecloth (muslin) and add to the bowl. Add the meat, turning to coat. Cover and refrigerate for at least 24 hours or for up to 2 days, turning occasionally.

Preheat the oven to 400°F (200°C). Remove the meat from the marinade, pat dry with paper towels, and season with salt and pepper. Strain the marinade and reserve the onion and garlic in one bowl and the liquid in another. Discard the remaining solids.

Place a large Dutch oven over high heat. Add the meat and brown on all sides, 7–8 minutes total. Transfer to a plate. Add the onion and garlic from the marinade to the pan and sauté for 1–2 minutes. Then add the marinade liquid and bring to a boil. Boil for 3–4 minutes, skimming off any scum. Return the meat to the Dutch oven and add the broth and the whole garlic cloves. Roast, uncovered, until the meat is evenly browned on top, about 15 minutes. Reduce the temperature to 375°F (190°C), cover, and continue to roast for 1 hour longer.

Meanwhile, cut an x 1/4 inch (6 mm) deep in the stem end of each whole onion. When the meat has roasted for a total of 1 1/4 hours, arrange the whole onions, turnips, carrots, parsnips, and potatoes around it. Cover and roast until the meat and vegetables are easily pierced with a knife, about 1 hour longer.

Transfer the meat to a cutting board and loosely tent with aluminum foil. Let rest for 5–8 minutes. Transfer the vegetables to a bowl and loosely tent with aluminum foil. Spoon off the fat from the pan juices.

Snip the strings, cut the meat across the grain into thin slices and arrange on a warmed platter. Arrange the vegetables around the meat, drizzle with some of the pan juices, and serve.

Serves 10–12

1 bottle (24 fl oz/750 ml) full-bodied red wine

1/2 cup (4 fl oz/125 ml) Cognac

5 large cloves garlic, chopped

1 yellow onion, chopped

1 bay leaf

3 or 4 fresh rosemary sprigs

1/2 teaspoon peppercorns

1/2 teaspoon whole cloves

1 eye of round beef roast, 4 1/2–5 lb (2.25–2.5 kg)

Coarse salt and freshly ground pepper

1 1/2 cups (12 fl oz/375 ml) Beef Stock (page 288) or broth

8–10 cloves garlic, unpeeled

6 small onions, each 2 inches (5 cm) in diameter, peeled but left whole

3 turnips, peeled and quartered

3 large carrots, peeled and cut into 2-inch (5-cm) chunks

3 parsnips, peeled and cut into 2-inch (5-cm) chunks

6 Yukon Gold or other yellow-fleshed potatoes, cut lengthwise into sixths

Chilied Flank Steak

Flank steak, a flavorful but not-so-tender cut, benefits from an overnight marinade. Scoring the steak helps keep it from shrinking as it cooks. Top round, often sold as London broil, or skirt steak can be substituted for the flank steak.

1 flank steak, about 1½ lb (750 g)

⅓ cup (3 fl oz/80 ml) regular or spicy vegetable juice cocktail such as V-8 juice

⅓ cup (3 fl oz/80 ml) soy sauce

¼ cup (2 fl oz/60 ml) safflower oil

⅓ cup (2½ oz/75 g) firmly packed dark brown sugar

2 cloves garlic, minced

1 tablespoon chili powder

⅛ teaspoon ground cumin

Using a sharp knife, score the flank steak on both sides, cutting about ⅛ inch (3 mm) deep and forming a diamond pattern.

In a glass bowl, whisk together the vegetable juice cocktail, soy sauce, safflower oil, brown sugar, garlic, chili powder, and cumin to make a marinade. Pour half of the marinade into a shallow nonaluminum dish. Place the steak in the dish and pour the remaining marinade over the top. Cover and refrigerate for 24 hours. Remove from the refrigerator 30 minutes before grilling.

Prepare a hot fire for direct-heat cooking in a grill (see pages 8–9). Position the grill rack 4–6 inches (10–15 cm) above the fire.

Remove the steak from the marinade and set aside. Pour the marinade into a small saucepan and bring to a boil over medium heat. Boil for 1 minute, remove from the heat, and strain through a sieve into a clean bowl. Cover and set aside.

Place the steak on the grill rack. Cook, turning once, until done to your liking, about 4 minutes on each side for medium-rare. Transfer to a cutting board and cover loosely with aluminum foil. Let rest for 5 minutes.

Carve the steak on the diagonal across the grain into slices about ¼ inch (6 mm) thick. Arrange on a warmed platter or individual plates and serve. Pass the reserved boiled marinade as a sauce at the table.

Serves 4

Asian Skewered Lamb

A marinade containing lemongrass and five-spice powder (a blend of cinnamon, star anise, fennel seeds, Sichuan peppercorns, and cloves) gives these kabobs an exceptional flavor. Serve them with couscous studded with toasted pine nuts.

In a large nonaluminum bowl, stir together the yogurt, shallot, lemongrass or lemon zest, soy sauce, five-spice powder, and sesame oil. Mix well. Stir in the lamb cubes, cover, and refrigerate for 2 hours. Remove from the refrigerator 30 minutes before grilling.

Meanwhile, trim the ends of the zucchini, slice into $1/4$ inch rounds, and place in a small bowl. Add 2 teaspoons of the olive oil and the curry powder. Mix well. Place the tomatoes in another bowl and add the remaining 1 teaspoon olive oil and the basil. Mix well.

Prepare a hot fire for direct-heat cooking in a grill (see pages 8–9). Position the rack 4–6 inches (10–15 cm) above the fire.

Divide the meat into 4 equal portions; you should have 5 pieces per serving. Onto each of 4 metal skewers, thread the ingredients in the following order: lamb, zucchini, lamb, tomato, lamb, zucchini, lamb, tomato, lamb.

Place the skewers on the grill rack. Cook, turning once, until nicely browned and done to your liking, 5–6 minutes on each side for medium-rare.

Transfer the skewers to individual plates and serve hot.

Serves 4

1 cup (8 oz/250 g) plain yogurt

1 shallot, minced

1 tablespoon minced lemongrass or 1$1/2$ teaspoons grated lemon zest

1 tablespoon soy sauce

2 teaspoons five-spice powder

1 teaspoon Asian sesame oil

2 lb (1 kg) boneless lamb from the leg, cut into 1$1/4$-inch (3-cm) cubes (20 cubes)

4 small zucchini (courgettes), each about 1 inch (2.5 cm) in diameter

3 teaspoons olive oil

$1/2$ teaspoon curry powder

8 cherry tomatoes

1 teaspoon chopped fresh basil

Smoked Brisket with Spicy Soppin' Sauce

The following recipe is based on an old Texas formula. Using water during the smoking process is mandatory here. It's the only way to come close to "real" barbecue at home. Serve with small roasted potatoes and corn bread on the side.

1 clove garlic, minced

1 teaspoon salt

1 teaspoon freshly ground pepper

1 tablespoon ground mild dried chile such as New Mexico

1 beef brisket, about 4 lb (2 kg)

FOR THE SPICY SOPPIN' SAUCE:

1 small dried hot chile

1 shallot

1 cup (8 fl oz/250 ml) cider vinegar

2 tablespoons brown sugar

1 tablespoon Worcestershire sauce

1 teaspoon ground coriander

1/2 teaspoon salt

1/2 teaspoon aniseed

1/4 teaspoon ground cumin

2 cups (16 fl oz/500 ml) tomato ketchup

Dash of hot-pepper sauce

In a small bowl, with the back of a heavy spoon, mash the garlic with the salt, pepper, and ground chile. Rub this spice mixture thoroughly into the meat on all sides. Place in a nonaluminum dish, cover, and refrigerate for 24 hours. Remove from the refrigerator 45 minutes before smoking.

Prepare a low-heat fire for indirect-heat cooking on a covered grill (see pages 8–9). Put the drip pan in place and fill the pan with water. Position the rack in the highest position above the fire. Place the brisket on the grill rack. Cover and cook, keeping the temperature between 190°F (88°C) and 225°F (110°C), until the meat is tender enough to cut with a fork, 6–7 hours. (Add more water to the pan as needed and, if using a charcoal smoker, more preheated coals to the fire pan as required.)

Meanwhile, make the sauce: In a food processor, combine the chile, shallot, vinegar, brown sugar, Worcestershire sauce, coriander, salt, aniseed, and cumin. Process until smooth. Transfer to a saucepan and stir in the ketchup. Bring to a boil over medium-high heat, reduce the heat to low, cover partially, and simmer, stirring occasionally, until the sauce has thickened, about 30 minutes. Season with the hot-pepper sauce. Set aside.

When the brisket is tender, transfer it to a cutting board and cover loosely with aluminum foil. Let stand for 15 minutes. Using a sharp knife, slice the meat across the grain or, using 2 forks, pull apart into chunks. Arrange on a warmed platter. Reheat the sauce over low heat, pour it into a bowl, and pass at the table.

Serves 6

Shredded Beef with Avocado-Tomatillo Salsa

Beef cooked with chiles and oregano for several hours becomes pleasantly spicy and so soft it can be shredded effortlessly with a fork. Serve on warmed tortillas, and accompany with a salad of crisp romaine (cos) lettuce and a bowl of black beans.

Preheat the oven to 325°F (165°C).

Rub the roast with the salt and pepper. Place in a heavy ovenproof baking dish with a tight-fitting lid. Crumble the ancho chiles over the roast and add the onion halves, garlic, and oregano. Cover and place in the oven. Cook until the meat is juicy and shreds easily with a fork, about 5 hours.

Just before the beef is ready, make the salsa: Bring a saucepan three-fourths full of water to a boil. Add the tomatillos and parboil until softened, about 5 minutes. Drain and let cool. Mince the tomatillos and place in a bowl. Add the chiles, cilantro, onion, garlic, and salt. Stir to combine. Halve, pit and peel the avocados. Using a fork, mash the avocado halves into the tomatillo mixture. The salsa should be a little chunky. Stir in the lime juice and check the seasonings.

Remove the meat from the oven and discard the onions. Using a fork, shred the beef in the dish, blending it with the juices. Keep warm until ready to serve, or refrigerate when cool. Reheat over low heat to serve.

Serve the beef warm with the salsa.

Serves 4–6

1 tri-tip or boneless chuck roast, 2 lb (1 kg)

1 teaspoon salt

1 teaspoon freshly ground pepper

4 ancho chiles

2 yellow onions, halved

4 cloves garlic, crushed

1 tablespoon fresh oregano leaves

FOR THE SALSA:

20 tomatillos, husks removed

6 Hungarian wax chiles, seeded and minced

4 serrano chiles, seeded and minced

1/4 cup (1/3 oz/10 g) chopped fresh cilantro (fresh coriander)

1/4 cup (1 1/2 oz/45 g) minced yellow onion

2 cloves garlic, minced

1/2 teaspoon salt

3 avocados

Juice of 4 limes (about 2 tablespoons)

Steak au Poivre with Oven Fries

You can find jars of mixed peppercorns (usually black, white, pink, and green) in many supermarket spice racks. Or, make your own blend of black, white, and green peppercorns to flavor this classic treatment for New York strip steak.

2 tablespoons mixed peppercorns (see note)

4 New York steaks, each about 3/4 lb (375 g)

3 tablespoons olive oil

4 russet potatoes, each about 1/2 lb (250 g)

Salt

In a mortar or in a spice grinder, grind the peppercorns coarsely. Brush the steaks on both sides with 1 1/2 tablespoons of the olive oil, then press the peppercorns into both sides of the steaks, coating evenly. Let stand at room temperature for 1 hour.

Preheat an oven to 450°F (230°C). Cut the potatoes in half lengthwise, then cut each half lengthwise into thirds to make 24 large fries total. Put the potato wedges in a bowl with cold water to cover and swish to remove the surface starch. Drain and refill the bowl with cold water. Let the potatoes stand in the water for 5 minutes longer, then swish again, drain well, and pat dry with a clean kitchen towel.

Put a heavy-duty baking sheet in the oven to preheat for 5 minutes. Meanwhile, coat the potato wedges with the remaining 1 1/2 tablespoons olive oil and sprinkle with salt to taste. When the baking sheet is hot, arrange the potatoes on it, one cut side down. Bake until the bottom sides are browned, 10–15 minutes. Turn to the other cut sides and continue baking until the other sides are browned and the potatoes are tender when pierced with a knife, 5–10 minutes longer.

While the potatoes are baking, place a frying pan over medium heat. Season the steaks with salt. When the frying pan is hot, add the steaks and cook, turning once, until done to your liking, 2–3 minutes on each side for medium-rare. Transfer to a cutting board and let stand for 10 minutes.

Slice the steaks on the diagonal and transfer the slices to a warmed plate, spoon any accumulated juices over them. Serve immediately with the potatoes.

Serves 4

Porterhouse Steak with Sauce Rouille

Trim the fat from the edges of the steak, leaving a layer $^1/_4$ inch (6 mm) thick, then slash the layer of fat at 1-inch (2.5-cm) intervals.

In a small bowl, mix together the garlic, anchovy paste, olive oil, and pepper. Rub into both sides of the steak. Cover and let stand at room temperature for 1 hour.

Meanwhile, make the sauce rouille: in a saucepan over medium-low heat, combine the potato and chicken broth. Bring to a simmer and cook, uncovered, until barely tender, about 10 minutes. Add the bell pepper and cook until heated through, about 3 minutes longer. Drain, reserving the broth; you should have 2–3 tablespoons.

In a food processor, chop the garlic, cherry peppers, pimientos, potato and bell pepper, thyme, vinegar, and hot-pepper sauce. With the motor running, slowly add the oil and process until the mixture thickens. Transfer to a bowl and whisk in the reserved broth. Season to taste with salt and pepper. Cover and refrigerate until serving.

Prepare a hot fire for direct-heat cooking in a grill (see pages 8–9) Position a grill rack 4–6 inches (10–15 cm) above the fire.

Place the steak on the grill rack and cook, turning once, until nicely browned, about 1 minute on each side. Reduce the heat to medium-high (you can move the steak to the edge of the coals or raise the grill rack), turning once, until done to your liking, 16–20 minutes total for medium-rare. Transfer to a cutting board and cover loosely with aluminum foil. Let stand for 5 minutes.

Cut the meat from the bone, then slice the meat across the grain and serve on a warmed platter. Pass the sauce at the table.

Serves 6

1 Porterhouse steak, 2$^1/_2$–3 lb (1.25–1.5 kg)

1 clove garlic, minced

1 teaspoon anchovy paste

2 teaspoons olive oil

$^1/_4$ teaspoon freshly ground pepper

FOR THE SAUCE ROUILLE:

1 russet potato, about 5 oz (155 g), peeled and chopped

$^1/_2$ cup (4 fl oz/125 ml) Chicken Stock (page 288) or broth

1 small red bell pepper (capsicum), seeded and chopped

3 cloves garlic, minced

3 jarred hot cherry peppers, drained and stems removed

1 jar (2 oz/60 g) chopped pimiento peppers, drained

$^1/_4$ teaspoon chopped fresh thyme

$^1/_4$ teaspoon red wine vinegar

Dash of hot-pepper sauce

5 tablespoons (2$^1/_2$ fl oz/75 ml) olive oil

Salt and freshly ground pepper

Veal Stuffed with Spring Greens

Place the veal in a shallow nonaluminum dish. Pour the milk over the meat and turn to coat well. Cover and refrigerate for at least 3 hours or for up to 24 hours. Discard the milk, rinse the roast, and pat dry with paper towels. Using a sharp knife, make a horizontal cut through the center of the meat and open it out flat. Rub with pepper and nutmeg to taste. Bring to room temperature, about 30 minutes.

Meanwhile, in a food processor, combine the arugula, mâche, watercress, and parsley and pulse to chop evenly but coarsely. In a large sauté pan over medium heat, melt the butter with 1 tablespoon of the oil. Add the shallots and sauté until soft, about 3 minutes. Add the chives and sauté until soft, about 1 minute longer. Add the chopped greens and sauté for 1 minute. Add the spinach and sauté until wilted, about 2 minutes longer. Season to taste with nutmeg, salt, and pepper and mix well. Let cool.

Preheat the oven to 400°F (200°C). Spread the stuffing over the cut side of the meat, then roll up to enclose. Using kitchen string, tie securely at intervals 2–3 inches (5–7.5 cm) apart. Place a Dutch oven on the stovetop over high heat and add the remaining 1 tablespoon olive oil. Add the veal and brown on all sides, 4–5 minutes total. Scatter the green onions around the meat, cover, and roast for 20 minutes.

In a small saucepan, bring the wine and stock to a simmer. Remove from the heat. After the roast has been cooking for 20 minutes, pour the hot wine mixture over the meat. Reduce the oven temperature to 350°F (180°C) and continue to cook, covered, basting every 10 minutes, until an instant-read thermometer inserted into the center registers 165°F (74°C), about 1 hour longer. Transfer to a cutting board, and let rest for 15 minutes. Boil the pan juices until reduced by one-half, about 8 minutes. Adjust the seasonings and strain into a warmed bowl. Slice the meat across the grain and transfer to a warmed platter. Pass the pan juices.

Serves 6–8

1 boneless veal roast cut from the leg, 4 lb (2 kg), trimmed

4 cups (32 fl oz/1 l) milk

Freshly ground pepper

Freshly grated nutmeg

1 cup (1 oz/30 g) *each* arugula (rocket), mâche, and watercress leaves, tough stems removed

1/2 bunch fresh flat-leaf (Italian) parsley, tough stems removed

2 tablespoons unsalted butter

2 tablespoons olive oil, or as needed

2 large shallots, minced

1 bunch fresh chives, minced

2 cups (2 oz/60 g) baby spinach leaves, tough stems removed

Coarse salt and freshly ground pepper

18 green (spring) onions, including 1 inch (2.5 cm) of the green tops, chopped

1/2 cup (4 fl oz/125 ml) *each* dry white wine and Veal Stock (page 289)

Grilled Peppery Rib-Eye Steak with Roquefort Butter

Pungent Blue cheese paired with a perfectly cooked peppered steak are a staple bistro dish. Serve with a simple green salad, French fries, and a robust red wine, and you will have an ideal menu for a dinner with friends.

To make the Roquefort butter, in a small food processor, combine the cheese, butter, Cognac to taste (if using), and the $^1/_2$ teaspoon pepper. Process to until blended. Remove from the processor, shape into a log, and wrap in plastic wrap. Refrigerate until needed. Bring to room temperature before serving.

In a small bowl, stir together the garlic, coarsely ground pepper, and enough olive oil to form a thick paste. Place the steaks in a nonaluminum dish and rub the paste evenly into both sides of the steaks. Let stand at room temperature for at least 1 hour or refrigerate for up to 6 hours. If refrigerated, bring to room temperature before grilling.

Prepare a hot fire for direct-heat cooking in a charcoal grill (pages 8–9) or preheat a broiler (grill). If using a grill, position a grill rack 4–6 inches (10–15 cm) above the fire.

Place the steaks on the grill rack, or place on a rack in a broiler pan and place under the broiler. Grill or broil, turning once, until done to your liking, 3–4 minutes on each side for medium-rare.

Transfer the steaks to a cutting board and let rest for 5 minutes. Cut the steaks away from the bone, if present, then slice the meat across the grain.

Transfer the sliced steaks to warmed individual plates. Cut the Roquefort butter into equal pieces and place a piece on each steak. Serve immediately.

Serves 4

FOR THE ROQUEFORT BUTTER:

2 oz (60 g) Roquefort, Gorgonzola, or other blue-veined cheese

$^1/_4$ cup (2 oz/60 g) unsalted butter, at room temperature

1–2 tablespoons Cognac (optional)

$^1/_2$ teaspoon freshly ground pepper

2 teaspoons finely minced garlic

$1^1/_2$ teaspoons coarsely ground pepper

About 2 tablespoons olive oil

4 well-marbled rib-eye, porterhouse, or New York strip steaks, each 8–10 oz (250–315 g) and 1 inch (2.5 cm) thick

Smoky Southwestern Veal Chops

Chipotle chiles impart their unique character to veal chops before they are smeared with a hot seasoning paste. Hulled green pumpkin seeds, also known as pepitas, are sold in Mexican markets and health-food stores.

6 loin veal chops, each
6–7 oz (185–220 g) and 1 inch
(2.5 cm) thick, trimmed of fat
and edges scored

2 chipotle chiles

About 2¹/₂ cups (20 fl oz/
625 ml) milk

1 dried árbol chile

1 dried Anaheim chile

1 dried ancho chile

1 teaspoon coarse salt, plus a
pinch

About 2 tablespoons
vegetable oil

1 large yellow onion, chopped

2 large cloves garlic, minced

¹/₂ bunch fresh cilantro (fresh
coriander), tough stems
removed chopped

¹/₃ cup (3 fl oz/80 ml) Veal
Stock (page 289) warmed

1 cup (8 oz/250 g) hulled green
pumpkin seeds (see note),
toasted

Place the veal chops and chipotle chiles in a large lock-top bag or dish. Pour in enough milk just to cover the meat. Seal the bag securely, or cover the dish. Refrigerate for at least 3 hours or up to 24 hours. Discard the milk and chiles, rinse the chops, and pat dry with paper towels.

Preheat the oven to 400°F (200°C). Using metal tongs, pass the árbol, Anaheim, and ancho chiles, one at a time over a flame on a gas stove to toast briefly, being careful not to blacken them. Place in a mortar all the toasted chiles with 1 teaspoon coarse salt, and use a pestle to grind until coarsely crushed. Rub the mixture into both sides of each chop and set aside.

In a large frying pan over medium-high heat, warm the oil. Add the chops and cook, turning once, until browned about 4 minutes on each side. Transfer to a plate. Reduce the heat to medium and add the onion and garlic. Cook, stirring often, until they begin to soften, about 6 minutes. Stir in the cilantro. Transfer the onion-cilantro mixture to a baking dish large enough to hold the chops in a single layer. Place the chops, along with any accumulated juices, on the onion-cilantro mixture and pour the stock around the meat. Roast until the chops are tender and the juices run clear when the chops are pierced with a knife, 12–14 minutes.

When the chops are ready, transfer them and the onion-cilantro mixture to a warmed platter. Sprinkle with the pumpkin seeds and serve immediately.

Serves 6

Tarragon Beef Fillet with Madeira and Mushroom Sauce

Preheat the oven to 500°F (260°C). Lightly oil a rimmed baking sheet. Rub the beef fillet with the tarragon and pepper. Fold the thin tail of meat under to make an evenly thick roast. Tie the meat with kitchen string at 2-inch intervals and place on the prepared baking sheet. Drizzle the Madeira over the beef and let marinate at room temperature for 30 minutes before roasting.

Place the fillet in the oven. Immediately reduce the heat to 450°F (230°C). Roast the meat until an instant-read thermometer inserted into the center of the meat registers for rare or for medium rare, 25–30 minutes. When the beef is ready, transfer it to a large sheet of parchment paper and roll it up. Next, enclose the meat in several sheets of newspaper. Let rest for 20–25 minutes.

Meanwhile, prepare the sauce: Squeeze the water from the rehydrated mushrooms. Remove and discard any tough stems and thinly slice the tops. In a large sauté pan over high heat, warm the olive oil. Working in batches, sauté each variety of dried and fresh mushroom separately, until they no longer give off any moisture, 4–5 minutes for each batch. Add a splash of Madeira in the last minute of sautéing each batch, season with salt and pepper, and transfer to a bowl.

Return the sauté pan to medium heat and melt the butter. Add the shallots and a little oil if needed, and sauté until soft, about 7 minutes. Season with the tarragon and pepper. Add the remaining Madeira and bring to a boil. Cook for 3 minutes. Return the mushrooms and their juices to the pan, add the stock, and bring to a boil. Reduce the heat to low and simmer, uncovered, until the liquid is reduced by half, about 20 minutes. Adjust the seasonings. Transfer to a warmed sauceboat.

To serve, unwrap the beef, and cut across the grain into slices. Arrange on a warmed platter, spoon on a bit of the sauce. Serve, passing the remaining sauce at the table.

Serves 8–10

1 whole beef fillet, 3–3½ lb (1.5–1.75 kg), trimmed

1 teaspoon dried tarragon

1 teaspoon freshly ground pepper

About 2 tablespoons Madeira wine

FOR THE MUSHROOM SAUCE:

6 dried shiitake mushrooms, soaked in warm water to cover for 30 minutes

1 oz (30 g) dried porcini or morel mushrooms, soaked in warm water to cover for 30 minutes

About 2 tablespoons olive oil

8 fresh oyster mushrooms, brushed clean and tough stems removed, sliced

6 oz (185 g) fresh button mushrooms, brushed clean and sliced

⅓ cup (3 fl oz/80 ml) Madeira wine

Salt and freshly ground pepper

2 tablespoons unsalted butter

4 shallots, chopped

1 tablespoon chopped fresh tarragon

1 cup (8 fl oz/250 ml) Beef Stock (page 288)

Flank Steak, Haricot Vert, and Potato Salad

Place an extra steak over the coals when you prepare Grilled Flank Steak with Horseradish (page 141) and serve this salad the next day. Corn on the cob and sliced tomatoes with basil round out the menu for a casual outdoor lunch.

FOR THE DRESSING:

¼ cup (2 fl oz/60 ml) red wine vinegar

¼ cup (1½ oz/45 g) minced shallot

2 teaspoons Dijon mustard

1 teaspoon *each* salt and freshly ground pepper

½ cup (4 fl oz/125 ml) olive oil

FOR THE SALAD:

⅔ lb (315 g) haricot verts, trimmed and left whole

2 lb (1 kg) red potatoes, unpeeled

2½ teaspoons chopped fresh thyme leaves

2 teaspoons chopped fresh rosemary leaves

Salt and freshly ground pepper

1 lb (500 g) flank steak, grilled (see note), at room temperature

6 tablespoons (2 oz/60g) crumbled blue cheese

To make the dressing, in a small bowl, whisk together the vinegar, shallot, mustard, salt and pepper. Whisk in the olive oil. (The dressing can be made up to 3 hours ahead. Cover and let stand at cool room temperature.)

Bring a large pot of lightly salted water to a boil. Add the beans and boil until just tender, 3–4 minutes. Using a slotted spoon, scoop out the beans and place under cold running water to halt the cooling and set the color. Pat dry with paper towels and set aside.

Return the water to a boil and add the potatoes. Boil until easily pierced with a sharp knife, 15–20 minutes. Drain. (The beans and potatoes can be prepared up to 3 hours ahead. Cover and keep at cool room temperature.)

When cool enough to handle, cut the cooked potatoes into 1-inch (2.5-cm) cubes. Place them in a large nonaluminum bowl along with the beans. Whisk the dressing and pour two-thirds of it over the potatoes and beans. Sprinkle with the thyme, rosemary, and salt and pepper to taste and mix well.

Slice the steak against the grain into slices ½ inch (6mm) thick, then cut each slice in half lengthwise.

To serve, divide the potato and bean mixture evenly among 6 individual plates. Divide the steak strips and mound in the center of each portion. Drizzle the meat with the remaining dressing, sprinkle each serving with 1 tablespoon blue cheese, and serve immediately.

Serves 6

Leg of Lamb with Lemon-Bay Marinade

Marinated and grilled lamb is an easy main course to prepare and serve outdoors, as it moves directly from the grill to the table and your waiting guests. Serve with Rustic Grilled Potatoes (page 231) and a fruity dry rosé for a convivial summer dinner.

In a shallow, nonaluminum dish or bowl large enough to hold the lamb, combine the olive oil, lemon juice, garlic, bay leaves, thyme, peppercorns, coriander seeds, and salt. Stir to mix well. Add the lamb and turn to coat well. Cover and refrigerate for 12–24 hours, turning the lamb from time to time.

Prepare a medium-hot fire for direct-heat cooking in a grill (see pages 8–9). Position the grill rack about 8 inches (20 cm) about the fire. Remove the lamb from the marinade, discard the marinade, and place on the grill rack. Grill until deeply browned on the first side, about 10 minutes, being careful the meat does not burn. Turn and grill until deeply browned on the second side, or until an instant-read thermometer inserted into the thickest part of the leg registers 135°F (57°C) for medium-rare or 145°F (63°C) for medium, 20–25 minutes longer. Transfer the lamb to a cutting board or platter and cover loosely with aluminum foil. Let rest for 10 minutes. While the lamb is resting, grill the lemon slices over the hottest part of the grill until lightly charred, about 1 minute on each side.

To serve, cut the lamb across the grain into thin slices and arrange with the grilled lemon slices on a warmed platter. Serve immediately, spooning some of the accumulated juices over each portion.

Serves 8–10

2/3 cup (5 fl oz/160 ml) olive oil

Juice of 3 lemons

8 cloves garlic, bruised

2 bay leaves

2 tablespoons fresh thyme leaves or 8 thyme sprigs, each 6 inches (15 cm) long

2 tablespoons peppercorns, bruised

2 tablespoons coriander seeds, bruised

1½ teaspoons salt

1 leg of lamb, 6–7 lb (3–3.5 kg), boned and butterflied

3 lemons, thinly sliced

Fast Mustard Lamb Chops

This recipe is for the person who loves good food but has little time to cook. The succulent, tender loin lamb chops roast in only 10 minutes. Serve with quick-cooking couscous laced with toasted pine nuts and sprinkled with chives.

8 small loin lamb chops, each 4–5 oz (125–155 g) and 1–1¼ inches (2.5–3 cm) thick, trimmed of fat and edges scored

Freshly ground pepper

About 4–5 tablespoons grainy Dijon mustard

Fresh flat-leaf (Italian) parsley sprigs for garnish (optional)

Preheat the oven to 500°F (260°C). Lightly oil a shallow roasting pan.

Rub both sides of each chop with pepper to taste and place in the prepared roasting pan. Slather about 1 teaspoon mustard on one side of each chop and bring to room temperature, 10–15 minutes.

Roast, mustard side up, until the chops are browned on top, about 5 minutes. Turn the chops over and spread about 1 teaspoon mustard on the second side. Continue to roast until the meat is pink in the center when cut into it with a knife, about 5 minutes longer for medium-rare, or until done to your liking. The roasting time will depend upon the thickness of the chops and personal preference.

Divide the chops among warmed individual plates, placing 2 chops on each plate. Garnish with the parsley and serve immediately.

Serves 4

Mint and Chive–Marinated Leg of Lamb

Make 15–20 small slits at regular intervals in the lamb. Remove 15–20 small leaves from the mint sprigs and insert into the slits. Bruise 6–8 of the mint sprigs. Place the lamb in a large, nonaluminum dish. Add the garlic, half of the ramps, the chives, the bruised mint sprigs, the peppercorns, and 1 cup (8 fl oz/250 ml) of the wine; turn the meat to coat evenly. Cover and refrigerate for at least 6 hours or for up to 3 days, turning occasionally. Bring to room temperature before roasting.

Preheat an oven to 450°F (230°C). Remove the meat from the marinade and pat dry with paper towels. Pour the marinade into a small saucepan, bring to a boil, then remove from the heat. Rub the lamb with salt and ground pepper. In a roasting pan over high heat, warm enough olive oil to form a film on the pan bottom. Add the lamb and brown on all sides, 5–6 minutes total. Arrange the the remaining ramps and a sprig or two of mint around the lamb in the roasting pan.

Roast for 15 minutes. Reduce the temperature to 375°F (190°C) and continue to roast, basting every 10–15 minutes with the reserved marinade, until an instant-read thermometer inserted into the thickest portion of the leg, away from the bone, registers 125°–130°F (52°–54°C) for medium-rare, about 35 minutes longer. Transfer to a cutting board, loosely tent with aluminum foil, and let rest for 10 minutes before carving.

Meanwhile, place the pan over high heat. Add the remaining 1 cup (8 fl oz/250 ml) wine and deglaze the pan, stirring to remove any browned bits from the pan bottom. Bring to a boil and boil until reduced by half, 5–8 minutes. Spoon off the fat from the juices, then strain through a fine-mesh sieve into a warmed sauceboat. Carve meat across the grain into slices. Arrange on a warmed platter and garnish with the remaining mint sprigs. Serve, passing the pan juices at the table.

Serves 8–10

1 leg of lamb, 5–6 lb (2.5–3 kg), trimmed of fat

15–20 fresh mint sprigs

2 large cloves garlic, minced

12–16 ramps, chopped (see page 296)

1/2 bunch fresh chives, cut into 2-inch (5-cm) lengths

1 teaspoon peppercorns

2 cups (16 fl oz/500 ml) full-bodied white wine

Coarse salt and ground pepper

About 1–2 teaspoons olive oil

Swiss-Style Steak

Here, round steak is marinated in tomato juice, then roasted on a bed of basil-scented onions and ripe tomatoes. The resulting sauce has the character of a fresh salsa. Use the first cut of the top round, if possible, as it is the most tender.

1 top-round steak, first cut, 3–3¹/₂ lb (1.5–1.75 kg) and 1¹/₂ inches (4 cm) thick

2 cups (16 fl oz/500 ml) tomato juice

1 tablespoon plus 2 teaspoons dried basil

1 teaspoon freshly ground pepper, plus more as needed

6 cloves garlic, minced

2 yellow onions

Coarse salt and freshly ground pepper

1 tablespoon olive oil, plus more as needed

3 large tomatoes, seeded and chopped

¹/₂ bunch fresh flat-leaf (Italian) parsley, chopped, plus more for garnish

2 pinches sugar, or more as needed

Place the steak in a large nonaluminum dish. Add the tomato juice, 1 tablespoon basil, 1 teaspoon pepper, and 4 minced garlic cloves. Slice 1 of the onions and add it as well. Cover the dish and refrigerate for at least 12 hours or for up to 24 hours, turning occasionally.

Preheat the oven to 400°F (200°C).

Remove the steak from the marinade and season with salt and pepper. Discard the remaining marinade.

In a Dutch oven over high heat, warm the 1 tablespoon olive oil. Add the meat and sear on both sides until browned, about 4 minutes on each side. Remove from the heat.

Chop the remaining onion. Coat the bottom of a small saucepan with olive oil and place over medium heat. Add the chopped onion and the remaining minced garlic and sauté until the onion begins to soften, about 2 minutes. Add the tomatoes, 2 teaspoons basil, ¹/₂ bunch parsley, and the sugar, salt, and pepper to taste. Stir well and cook until the tomatoes begin to release their juices, 2–3 minutes. Remove from the heat and spoon the tomato mixture around the steak.

Place the steak in the oven and roast, uncovered, until the meat is tender and done to your liking, 25–30 minutes longer for medium-rare.

Remove the meat from the oven and cut it across the grain into thick slices. Arrange the slices on a warmed platter, spooning the tomato mixture alongside. Garnish with chopped parsley and serve immediately.

Serves 6

Leg of Lamb with Peppery Mint Jelly

A classic leg of lamb served with mint jelly is even more delectable when cooked on the grill. When choosing a bone-in leg of lamb, select a one-half or three-quarter leg weighing no more than 4 pounds (2 kg) to keep the grilling time to under 1½ hours.

Using the tip of a sharp knife, make small slits at regular intervals in the lamb. Sliver 1 of the garlic cloves and insert the slivers into the slits.

Smash the remaining garlic clove with the side of a heavy knife and mash the garlic to a coarse paste. Place in a small bowl. Add the mustard, olive oil, soy sauce, rosemary or thyme, and ginger and mix well. Spread the mixture over the lamb, coating evenly, and place in a nonaluminum dish. Refrigerate, uncovered, for 2 hours. Remove from the refrigerator 30 minutes before cooking.

Prepare a hot fire for indirect-heat cooking in a covered grill (see pages 8-9). Position the grill rack 4–6 inches (10–15 cm) above the fire. Place the lamb in the center of the grill rack so it's not directly over the fire. Cover the grill and position the vents three-quarters open. Cook until an instant-read thermometer inserted into the thickest part of the leg away from the bone registers 140°F (60°C) for medium-rare, about 1¼ hours, adding more coals if necessary after the first 45 minutes of cooking to maintain a constant temperature.

Meanwhile, make the jelly: In a bowl, whisk together the apple-mint and jalapeño jellies and the wine vinegar until smooth. Whisk in the mint. Store tightly covered in the refrigerator until ready to serve.

When the lamb is done, transfer to a cutting board, tent loosely with aluminum foil, and let stand for about 15 minutes. Carve the meat across the grain into slices, arrange on a warmed platter, and serve immediately. Pass the mint jelly at the table.

Serves 4–6

1 shank-end or sirloin half partial bone-in leg of lamb, about 4 lb (2 kg) (see note)

2 cloves garlic

½ cup (4 oz/125 g) Dijon mustard

2 tablespoons olive oil

2 tablespoons soy sauce

½ teaspoon chopped fresh rosemary or thyme

½ teaspoon ground ginger

FOR THE PEPPERY MINT JELLY:

1 jar (12 oz/375 g) apple-mint jelly

¼ cup (3 oz/90 g) jalapeño jelly

1 tablespoon white wine vinegar

¼ cup (⅓ oz/10 g) chopped fresh mint

French-Style Steaks with Skewers of Rosemary-Scented Morels

Slices of boneless rib-eye steak are an excellent choice to accompany the woodsy flavor of morel mushrooms. The mushrooms are threaded on to stiff rosemary branches to grill, imparting an further aromatic, herbaceous quality.

24 fresh morel mushrooms, brushed clean

4 fresh woody rosemary branches, each about 8 inches (20 cm) long

1 teaspoon freshly ground pepper, plus more as needed

3/4 teaspoon salt, plus more as needed

2 tablespoons unsalted butter, cut into bits

4 boneless rib-eye steaks, each about 1/3 lb (155 g) and 1/2 inch (12 mm) thick

Prepare a medium-hot fire for direct-heat cooking in a grill (see pages 8–9). Position a grill rack 4–6 inches (10–15 cm) above the fire.

Cut a slit in the center of each morel, then thread the morels onto the rosemary branches, dividing them evenly. (Alternatively, use wooden skewers, first soaking them in water to cover for 30 minutes.) Sprinkle the mushrooms with the 1 teaspoon pepper and the 3/4 teaspoon salt and dot with the butter. Lay a 12-inch (30-cm) square of heavy-duty aluminum foil on a work surface and place the rosemary branches (or skewers) with the mushrooms on it in a single layer.

Place the aluminum foil on the grill rack and grill, turning the branches or skewers often, just until the mushrooms are cooked through, 3–4 minutes. Remove from the grill. Keep the mushrooms warm until the steaks are grilled.

Place the steaks on the rack over the fire and grill, turning once, until done to your liking, 2–3 minutes on each side for medium-rare, 3–5 minutes on each side for medium. Season with salt and pepper and transfer to 4 individual plates. Top each steak with a morel skewer and serve immediately.

Serves 4

Grilled Flank Steak with Horseradish Mashed Potatoes

Flank steak has a rich flavor and it is relatively inexpensive. That means you can serve a tasty steak dinner to your friends without breaking the bank. Ask one of your friends to supervise the grilling as you make the mashed potatoes.

Place the steak in a shallow nonaluminum dish. In a small bowl, stir together the garlic, vinegar, olive oil, and thyme. Brush the mixture on both sides of the steak, cover, and refrigerate for at least 2 hours or for up to 24 hours. Bring to room temperature before grilling.

Prepare a hot fire for direct-heat cooking in a charcoal grill (see pages 8–9). Position the grill rack 4–5 inches (10–13 cm) above the fire.

To cook the potatoes, bring a saucepan three-fourths full of lightly salted water to a boil. Add the potatoes and cook until easily pierced with a sharp knife, about 15 minutes. Drain well and place in a bowl. Add the cheese, 1/2 cup milk, horseradish, butter, mustard, 1/2 teaspoon salt and scant 1/2 teaspoon pepper. Using an electric mixer at low speed, beat just until the ingredients are incorporated. Taste and add additional horseradish if needed, then taste again and adjust the seasonings. If the potatoes are too thick, thin by beating in a small amount of additional warm milk. Cover loosely with aluminum foil until serving.

Just before the potatoes are ready to drain, put the steak on the oiled grill rack. Grill, turning once, until done to your liking, 4–5 minutes on each side. Transfer the steak to a cutting board and season with salt and pepper. Let rest for 5 minutes.

To serve, thinly slice the meat against the grain. Arrange the slices, overlapping them, on a warmed platter along with the mashed potatoes. Garnish the meat with the thyme springs, if using, and sprinkle the potatoes with parsley. Serve immediately.

Serves 4

1 flank steak, 1 1/2 lb (750 g)

6 cloves garlic, finely chopped

2 tablespoons red wine vinegar

1 tablespoon olive oil

2 teaspoons dried thyme

FOR THE POTATOES:

2 lb (1 kg) Yukon gold potatoes, peeled and cut into 1-inch (2.5-cm) cubes

2/3 cup (2 1/2 oz/75g) shredded Gruyére cheese

About 1/2 cup (4 fl oz/125 ml) milk, heated

3 tablespoons prepared horseradish

1 1/2 tablespoons unsalted butter, at room temperature

1 1/2 teaspoons Dijon mustard

About 1/2 teaspoon *each* salt and freshly ground pepper

Salt and freshly ground pepper

Fresh thyme sprigs (optional)

1 tablespoon chopped fresh flat-leaf (Italian) parsley

Pork

Pork Satay with Bell Peppers

A heavy dose of coriander flavors this satay, giving the taste buds a real rush. Accompany these peanutty morsels with mashed sweet potatoes or saffron-scented couscous for a casual dinner, or make smaller skewers for a fun cocktail-party spread.

1 clove garlic

1 shallot

¼ cup (1¼ oz/37 g) dry-roasted peanuts

2 tablespoons ground coriander

1 tablespoon brown sugar

1 teaspoon salt

¼ teaspoon freshly ground black pepper

⅛ teaspoon cayenne pepper

¼ cup (2 fl oz/60 ml) soy sauce

3 tablespoons lemon juice

1½ lb (750 g) boneless lean pork loin, cut into 1-inch (2.5-cm) cubes

1 red bell pepper (capsicum), seeded and cut into 1-inch (2.5-cm) squares

1 green bell pepper (capsicum), seeded and cut into 1-inch (2.5-cm) squares

Turn on a food processor, drop the garlic clove and then the shallot through the feed tube, and process until minced. Add the peanuts, coriander, brown sugar, salt, black pepper, cayenne pepper, soy sauce, and lemon juice. Process until smooth. Transfer the mixture to a nonaluminum bowl and stir in the pork, coating evenly. Cover and refrigerate for at least 2 hours or for up to 6 hours. Remove from the refrigerator 30 minutes before grilling.

Prepare a hot fire for direct-heat cooking in a grill (see pages 8–9). Position the grill rack 4–6 inches (10–15 cm) above the fire.

Meanwhile, bring a saucepan three-fourths full of salted water to a boil. Add the bell peppers and parboil for 3 minutes. Drain, rinse under cold running water, and drain again.

Remove the pork from the marinade and divide into 4 equal portions. Thread the pork onto 4 metal skewers, alternating them with the pepper squares.

Place the skewers on the grill rack. Cook, turning frequently, until the pork and peppers are nicely browned and the pork is no longer pink when a cube is cut into with a knife, 8–10 minutes.

Transfer to warmed individual plates and serve immediately.

Serves 4

Grilled Pork Chops, Asian Pears, and Torpedo Onions

Asian pears, which come into farmers' markets in late summer and early autumn, make a fine accompaniment to sweet red onions and pork chops. Cooked together on the grill, this combination picks up a wonderfully smoky flavor.

Prepare a medium-hot fire for direct-heat cooking in a charcoal grill (see pages 8–9). Position the grill rack 4–6 inches (10–15 cm) above the fire.

Sprinkle the pork chops with 2 tablespoons of the sage leaves and $^1/_2$ teaspoon each of the salt and pepper. Set aside.

In a bowl, mix together the pears and onions and drizzle with the oil. Toss to coat. Add the remaining $^1/_2$ teaspoon each salt and pepper and 2 tablespoons sage. Stir to mix well. The onions will fall apart.

When the fire is medium-hot, place an oiled grilling basket on the grill rack to preheat it. When it is hot, place the onions and pears in it, close the basket, and grill until golden on the underside, 4–5 minutes. Turn over the basket and continue to cook until the pears and onion are golden on the second side and tender when pierced, 4–5 minutes longer. Remove the onions and pears from the basket, transfer to a warmed platter, and keep warm.

Place the pork chops on the grill rack and grill, turning once, until they are browned and the juices run clear when a chop is cut into with a knife, 3–4 minutes on each side. Remove the chops from the grill and let rest for 5 minutes.

Arrange the chops on the platter or warmed individual plates. Spoon the pears and onions on top or alongside and serve.

Serves 4

4 rib pork chops, each about 4 oz (125 g) and $^3/_4$ inch (2 cm) thick

4 tablespoons ($^1/_4$ oz/7 g) fresh sage leaves

1 teaspoon salt

1 teaspoon freshly ground pepper

3 Asian pears, peeled, halved, cored, and cut into wedges about $^1/_2$ inch (12 mm) thick

2 red torpedo onions, cut into wedges about $^1/_2$ inch (12 mm) thick

2 tablespoons canola oil

Grilled Chipotle-Marinated Pork

The slightly sweet-and-hot glaze gives this pork a full, delicious flavor with a distinctive smoky note of chipotle. Be sure not to overcook the pork or it will become tough and dry. Pork today can be safely eaten when it is still pale pink inside.

2 pork tenderloins, (10 oz/ 315 g) each, trimmed

3 canned chipotle chiles in adobo sauce, seeded

2 tablespoons lime juice

3 tablespoons honey

2 large cloves garlic

1 tablespoon soy sauce

2 teaspoons ground cumin

1/4 cup (1/3 oz/10 g) chopped fresh cilantro (fresh coriander), plus sprigs for garnish

Cut each tenderloin in half crosswise. Set aside. In a blender, combine the chipotle chiles, lime juice, honey, garlic, soy sauce, and cumin. Blend until smooth. Stir in the cilantro. Transfer half of the mixture to a shallow, nonaluminum bowl. Reserve the other half. Add the pork to the bowl and turn to coat, then cover and refrigerate for 4–6 hours. Bring pork to room temperature before grilling.

Prepare a medium-hot fire for direct-heat cooking in a grill (see pages 8–9). Position the grill rack about 6–8 inches (15–20 cm) above the fire.

Oil the grill rack. Remove the pork from the marinade and place on the grill rack. Cook until seared on the first side, about 4 minutes. Turn over the pork pieces and spoon the reserved chile mixture evenly on top. Tent them with aluminum foil. Continue to cook until the pork is just firm to the touch and pale pink when cut into at the thickest point, about 4 minutes longer.

Transfer the pork to a cutting board and let rest for about 7 minutes. Slice and arrange on warmed individual plates. Garnish with cilantro sprigs and serve hot.

Serves 4

Foil-Wrapped Stuffed Pork Chops

When the sealed packets are unfolded, each guest is greeted with the herb-infused chops. Vegetables such as bell peppers (capsicums), tomato halves, or sections of corn on the cob can be added to the foil packet.

2½ cups (5 oz/155 g) cubed day-old bread (1-inch/ 2.5-cm cubes), preferably coarse country bread

1–2 cups (8–16 fl oz/ 250–500 ml) milk

3 tablespoons minced yellow onion

2 tablespoons chopped fresh parsley

1 tablespoon minced fresh sage

2 teaspoons minced fresh thyme

1 teaspoon dried winter savory

½ teaspoon salt

½ teaspoon freshly ground pepper

4 large loin pork chops, each about 10 oz (315 g) and 1½ inches (4 cm) thick

½ teaspoon salt

½ teaspoon freshly ground pepper

Place the bread cubes in a bowl and pour in 1 cup (8 fl oz/250 ml) of the milk. Let stand until the bread is very soft and has absorbed the milk, about 15 minutes. If necessary, add up to 1 cup (8 fl oz/250 ml) more milk. When the bread is evenly moist, squeeze it dry and place in a clean bowl. Discard the milk. Add the onion, parsley, sage, thyme, winter savory, salt, and pepper to the bread and mix well.

Using a small, sharp knife, cut a horizontal slit 1 inch (2.5 cm) deep into the side of each pork chop. Working inward from the slit, cut almost to the opposite side of the chop; be careful not to cut through the chop completely. Spoon an equal amount of the stuffing into each chop. They will be quite full.

Sprinkle the ½ teaspoon salt into a wide, heavy frying pan and place over medium-high heat. When it is hot, add the pork chops and sear, turning once, until nicely browned on both sides, about 2 minutes on each side.

Cut 4 pieces of aluminum foil each large enough to wrap and seal a pork chop. Working wit 1 chop at a time, place it on a piece of foil, sprinkle with the pepper, and then fold in the ends of the foil, overlapping them. Bring the sides together and fold over to make a tight seal. Place the packets on a baking sheet and bake for 45–50 minutes. To test for doneness, open 1 foil packet and check that the stuffing is cooked through and the pork is opaque when cut into with a knife.

To serve, place a packets on each of 4 individual plates and serve, letting the diners open the packets at the table.

Serves 4

Mixed Sausages and Eggplant Grill

Hearty flavors and a simple preparation make this a good dish to serve to a crowd at a backyard barbecue. The eggplant can be marinated up to 1 hour in advance. Accompany with cold beer and assorted mustards.

Prepare a medium-hot fire for direct-heat cooking in a grill (see pages 8–9). Position the grill rack 4–6 inches (10–15 cm) above the fire.

Brush the eggplant slices on both sides with the olive oil. Place in a bowl or shallow baking dish. Add the thyme, pepper, and salt and toss to distribute evenly.

When the grill is ready, place the eggplant slices directly on the grill rack or in a grill basket on the rack. Grill until a golden crust forms on the first side, 7–8 minutes. Turn and grill on the second side until a golden crust forms, 6–7 minutes longer. Transfer to a platter and keep warm or let cool to room temperature.

Arrange the sausages on the grill rack or in a grill basket on the rack. Grill, turning often, until the juices run clear when the sausages are pierced with a knife, 10–15 minutes. Remove the sausages from the grill and arrange on one or more platters with the eggplant slices. Serve immediately.

Serves 6–8

2 or 3 eggplants (aubergines), cut crosswise into slices 1/2 inch (12 mm) thick

1/4 cup (2 fl oz/60 ml) olive oil

1 tablespoon fresh thyme leaves

1 teaspoon freshly ground pepper

1/4 teaspoon salt

12–18 assorted sausages, 3–4 1/2 lb (1.5–2.25 kg) total weight, such as mild Italian, chicken-apple, or bratwurst

Roast Pork Loin with Tarragon, Mustard, and Cream

Pork is known to be inherently sweet, a characteristic intensified by roasting and offset by the slight bite of the mustard cream sauce served with it. Accompany the pork loin with sautéed apples and cherries and fried or roasted potatoes.

1 bone-in pork loin, 3–4 lb (1.5–2 kg)

3 large cloves garlic, slivered

Salt and freshly ground pepper

1/4 cup (2 oz/60 g) unsalted butter

3 tablespoons minced shallot

1/2 cup (4 fl oz/125 ml) Chicken Stock (page 288), or broth

2–3 tablespoons strong Dijon mustard

1 cup (8 fl oz/250 ml) heavy (double) cream

2–3 tablespoons chopped fresh tarragon

Preheat the oven to 400°F (200°C).

With the tip of a sharp knife, cut 3/4-inch (2-cm) slits all over the pork loin. Insert the garlic slivers into the slits. Sprinkle the meat with salt and pepper to taste and place in a roasting pan.

Roast the pork until an instant-read thermometer inserted into the thickest part of the meat away from the bone registers 147°–150°F (64°–65°C) or the meat is pale pink when cut into at the thickest portion, about 1 hour. Transfer to a cutting board and let rest while you make the sauce.

In a sauté pan over low heat, melt the butter. Add the shallot and sauté slowly until soft, about 5 minutes. Add the chicken stock and let cook until almost totally evaporated, about 5 minutes. Whisk in 2 tablespoons of the mustard and the cream and simmer until the sauce is slightly thickened, about 5 minutes. Stir in 2 tablespoons of the tarragon and season with salt and pepper. Taste and adjust the seasonings with more mustard or tarragon. Remove from the heat and keep warm.

Carve the pork into individual chops and arrange on a warmed platter or individual plates. Spoon the sauce over the chops and serve immediately.

Serves 4

Apple-Roasted Pork Chops with Roast Applesauce

Place the chops in a large nonaluminum dish. Add 3/4 cup (6 fl oz/180 ml) of the cider, the olive oil, half of the onions, the thyme, garlic, and peppercorns. Cover and refrigerate for at least 4 hours, turning occasionally.

Preheat the oven to 400°F (200°C). Remove the chops from the marinade, pat dry with paper towels, and season with salt and pepper. Discard the marinade. In a large sauté pan over high heat, melt the butter with the olive oil. When the foam subsides, add the chops and sear, turning once, until browned, about 2 minutes on each side. Meanwhile, scatter the fresh and dried apples and remaining onion slices in a baking dish large enough to hold the chops in a single layer. Set the browned chops on top of the apple and onion, pour the remaining 1/4 cup (2 fl oz/60 ml) apple cider around the chops, and cover the dish.

In a large baking dish with a lid, combine the quartered apples, 3/4 cup (6 fl oz/180 ml) water, and a pinch of salt. Place both baking dishes in the oven. Roast for 10 minutes, then reduce the temperature to 350°F (180°C) and cover the baking dish holding the apples. Continue to roast until the chops arenearly tender, about 25 minutes longer. Uncover and baste with the Calvados. Continue to roast until the juices run clear when the meat is pierced with a knife, and the chops are tender, about 10 minutes longer. Turn the apples occasionally during roasting. They are ready when soft.

Remove both dishes from the oven. Working in batches, pass the roasted apple quarters through a food mill placed over a bowl; discard the skins and seeds. Add the sugar. Transfer the sauce to a warmed bowl and sprinkle the cinnamon on top.

Serve the pork chops directly from the dish. Pass the applesauce at the table.

Serves 6

6 loin pork chops, each 7–8 oz (220–250 g) and 1 inch (2.5 cm) thick, trimmed of fat and edges scored

1 cup (8 oz/250 ml) apple cider

1 teaspoon olive oil

2 yellow onions, sliced

1 tablespoon fresh thyme leaves

2 cloves garlic, minced

1 teaspoon peppercorns

Salt and freshly ground pepper

1 tablespoon unsalted butter

1 tablespoon olive oil, or as needed

2 tart green apples, peeled, cored, and sliced

1 generous cup (3 oz/90 g) dried apples

8–10 tart apples, half green and half red, quartered

1/4 cup (2 fl oz/60 ml) Calvados or other dry apple brandy

1/4 cup (2 oz/60 g) sugar

1/2 teaspoon ground cinnamon

Pork Chops with Roasted Shallot, Tomato, and Rosemary Relish

The relish improves in flavor if made 2 or 3 days before serving. You might even make a double batch and keep the second one on hand for a night when you don't feel like cooking; it also complements other meats, such as lamb or duck.

6 large shallots, halved

Salt and freshly ground black pepper

4 plum (Roma) tomatoes, seeded and chopped

¼ cup (⅓ oz/10 g) chopped fresh flat-leaf (Italian) parsley

1 tablespoon balsamic vinegar

1 tablespoon honey

2 teaspoons minced fresh rosemary, plus sprigs for garnish

¼ teaspoon cayenne pepper

4 boneless pork loin chops, 5 oz (155 g) each, trimmed

Preheat the oven to 400°F (200°C).

Place the shallots in a baking pan. Season with salt and pepper, and coat with nonstick cooking spray. Roast for 15 minutes. Turn over the shallots and continue to roast until soft, about 10 minutes longer. Remove from the oven, let cool, and chop coarsely.

In a bowl, combine the roasted shallots, tomatoes, parsley, vinegar, honey, minced rosemary, and cayenne. Season to taste with salt and pepper. Set aside, or cover and refrigerate for up to 3 days.

Heat a large frying pan over medium-high heat. Coat the pan with nonstick cooking spray. Season the pork chops with salt and black pepper. Add the chops to the pan and cook on the first side until well seared, about 4 minutes. Turn and continue to cook until pale pink when cut into at the thickest point, about 3 minutes longer.

Transfer the pork chops to a warmed platter and top with the relish, dividing evenly. Garnish with rosemary sprigs and serve hot.

Serves 4

Grilled Fontina and Prosciutto Sandwiches

Ordinary "grilled" cheese sandwiches become a special lunch for weekend visitors when you use an out-of-the-ordinary filling. Rich and creamy Italian Fontina, makes the most satisfying sandwich, as it has a slightly nutty taste and melts beautifully.

Place 4 slices of bread on a work surface. Divide the cheese evenly among them, top each with a slice of prosciutto, and then sprinkle with rosemary, again dividing evenly. Cover with the remaining bread slices.

In a large, heavy frying pan, pour in enough of the olive oil to form a film on the bottom, and place over medium-high heat. When hot, add as many sandwiches as will fit comfortably in the pan. Cook the sandwiches, pressing down often with a metal spatula, until golden brown on the bottoms, 2–3 minutes. Turn over the sandwiches, adding more oil to the pan if necessary to prevent scorching. Cook, again pressing down on the sandwiches, until golden brown on the second sides, about 2 minutes longer. Transfer to a plate and repeat with the remaining sandwiches, adding more oil to the pan as needed.

Cut the sandwiches on the diagonal. Garnish with the rosemary sprigs, if using. Serve hot.

Serves 4

8 large slices coarse country bread, each about 1/2 inch (12 mm) thick

5–6 oz (155–185 g) Italian Fontina cheese, perferably from Val d'Aosta, sliced

4 thin slices prosciutto, about 2 oz (60 g) total weight

2 teaspoons chopped fresh rosemary, or 1 1/2 teaspoons dried rosemary, plus 4 fresh sprigs (optional)

About 3 tablespoons olive oil

Baby Back Ribs with Peach Sauce

Some cooks like to parboil the ribs before saucing and finishing them on the grill. In this recipe, however, the ribs are cooked soley on the grill, at a low temperature. For added color, garnish the ribs with sliced peaches.

3 lb (1.5 kg) baby back ribs

2 lemons, halved

1 teaspoon freshly ground pepper

1/2 teaspoon salt

FOR THE PEACH SAUCE:

1 cup (12 oz/375 g) peach preserves

1 yellow onion, finely chopped

1/4 cup (2 oz/60 g) firmly packed brown sugar

1/4 cup (2 fl oz/60 ml) Worcestershire sauce

1/4 cup (2 fl oz/60 ml) cider vinegar

1 tablespoon tomato ketchup

1 teaspoon dry mustard

1 teaspoon Hungarian sweet paprika

1/4 teaspoon hot-pepper sauce

Rub the ribs thoroughly with the lemon halves. Then, rub them with the pepper and salt. Place in a shallow nonaluminum dish, cover, and refrigerate for 24 hours. Remove from the refrigerator 30 minutes before grilling.

Meanwhile, make the peach sauce: In a saucepan over medium-low heat, combine the peach preserves, onion, brown sugar, Worcestershire sauce, vinegar, ketchup, dry mustard, paprika, and hot-pepper sauce. Bring to a boil, stirring occasionally to dissolve the sugar, then reduce the heat to medium-low and simmer, uncovered, until slightly thickened, about 10 minutes. Remove from the heat and let cool. Pour about $^{1}/_{3}$ cup (3 fl oz/80 ml) of the sauce into a small bowl and reserve for basting.

Prepare a hot fire for indirect-heat cooking in a covered grill (see pages 8–9). Position the grill rack 4–6 inches (10–15 cm) above the fire.

Place the ribs in the center of the grill rack so it's not directly over the fire. Cover the grill and open the vents halfway. Cook the ribs until tender, about 1 hour. (If using a charcoal grill, add more preheated coals after 40 minutes of cooking to maintain a constant temperature.) When the ribs are tender, move them directly over the fire and continue to grill, uncovered, turning once and basting with some of the peach sauce, until crisp on both sides, about 4 minutes longer.

Cut the ribs into sections, place on a platter, and serve immediately. Pour the remaining peach sauce into a bowl and pass at the table.

Serves 4

Ginger Peach–Glazed Ham

The ham tastes great hot and at room temperature. It's ideal for a large gathering or buffet. For the best flavor, look for peach preserves made with just fruit and sugar, and no artificial ingredients.

Preheat an oven to 325°F (165°C). Using a sharp knife, cut 8 or 9 horizontal slits, each $^1/_8$–$^1/_4$ inch (3–6 mm) deep and running at an angle in the upper side of the ham. Slip the cinnamon-stick pieces into the slits, poking them into the meat.

Set the ham on a rack in a large roasting pan, cinnamon side up. Pour the wine into the pan and tent with aluminum foil, sealing the edges securely. Bake for 2 hours. Meanwhile, in a small saucepan over medium heat, combine the peach preserves, pickled ginger, dry ginger, and mustard. Stir well and heat until the preserves melt.

After 2 hours, remove the ham from the oven and replace any loose cinnamon sticks. Raise the oven temperature to 350°F (180°C). Stir about 2 tablespoons of the pan juices into the glaze to thin it. Then spoon about three-fourths of the thinned glaze over the ham. Sprinkle 2 tablespoons of the brown sugar on the glaze, then pat it with the back of a spoon so that it clings to the meat. Return the ham to the oven and continue baking for 1 hour.

Remove the ham from the oven and baste it with pan juices, and apply the remaining glaze and sugar. Continue to bake until the glaze is browned and bubbly and an instant-read thermometer inserted into the thickest part of the ham registers 140°F (60°C), about 30 minutes longer. Remove from the oven, tent loosely with foil, and let rest for 25 minutes.

Transfer the ham to a large platter. Beginning at the large end of the ham, carve across the grain into thin slices. Serve hot or at room temperature.

Serves 20-24

5 cinnamon sticks, each about 6 inches (15 cm) long, broken into 1$^1/_2$–2 inch (4–5 cm) pieces

1 precooked smoked ham, about 15 lb (7.5 kg)

2 cups (16 fl oz/500 ml) dry white wine

FOR THE PEACH GLAZE:

1 jar (15 oz/470 g) peach preserves

1 tablespoon minced pickled ginger

1$^1/_2$ teaspoons ground dry ginger

1 teaspoon dry mustard

4 tablespoons (2 oz/60 g) firmly packed light brown sugar

Pork Chops with Green Chile and Pecan Stuffing

4 double-thick pork chops, each about 3/4 lb (375 g)

2 teaspoons Hungarian sweet paprika

1 teaspoon salt

1/2 teaspoon freshly ground pepper

3 tablespoons unsalted butter

1 small yellow onion, chopped

1 small poblano chile, about 2 1/2 oz (75 g), roasted, peeled, seeded, and finely chopped

1 cup (2 oz/60 g) dried bread cubes (1/4-inch/6-mm cubes)

1/4 cup (1 oz/30 g) chopped pecans

1/4 cup (2 fl oz/60 ml) Chicken Stock (page 288), or broth

2 teaspoons olive oil

Working with 1 chop at a time, place it on a cutting board and, using a small, sharp knife, cut a horizontal slit in the middle of the side, extending it about halfway along the length of the chop. Work the knife back and forth into the meat to form a pocket 1 1/2 inches (4 cm) deep. Do not cut all the way through the meat. Sprinkle the chops inside and out with the paprika, salt, and pepper, place in a shallow dish, cover, and refrigerate for at least 2 hours. Remove from the refrigerator 15 minutes before stuffing.

In a saucepan over medium-low heat, melt the butter. Add the onion, cover, and cook, stirring occasionally, until softened, about 5 minutes. Stir in the poblano chile, bread cubes, and pecans, mixing well. Add the chicken stock and stir again. Remove from the heat.

Prepare a hot fire for direct-heat cooking in a covered grill (see pages 8–9). Position the grill rack 4–6 inches (10–15 cm) above the fire. At the same time, soak 8 wooden toothpicks in water to cover for at least 20 minutes.

Meanwhile, using a teaspoon, stuff the chops with the bread cube mixture, dividing it evenly. Drain the toothpicks and use them to secure the pockets closed. Brush each chop on both sides with 1/2 teaspoon oil.

Place the chops on the rack and sear on each side for 1 minute. Cover the grill and open the vents. Continue to cook the chops, turning once, until an instant-read thermometer inserted into the thickest part of a chop away from the bone registers 160°F (71°C), about 25 minutes. Transfer to warmed individual plates, remove the toothpicks, and serve.

Serves 4

Smoked Pork Loin
with Red Onion Confit

Place the rosemary leaves, chopped sage, sea salt, and peppercorns in a spice grinder and grind coarsely. Transfer to a small bowl, add 1 tablespoon of the olive oil, and stir to make a paste. Rub the pork loin with the remaining 1 tablespoon olive oil and then rub evenly with the paste.

Using 60–70 charcoal briquettes, prepare a hot fire in a kettle-style grill. When the coals are hot, spread them over the bottom of the grill and add another 12 briquettes. Position the grill rack 8–10 inches above the fire. Let burn for 2–3 minutes, then close the bottom vent. Place the pork loin on the grill rack. Cover and open the lid vent fully. Cook for 15 minutes, then turn and cook for another 15 minutes.

Remove the pork loin from the grill and lay the rosemary branches on the rack to form a bed. Place the roast on the branches, cover the grill, and open the bottom vent. Let the smoke rise in a steady stream through the lid vent for about 5 minutes, then close the bottom vent. Cook for 10 minutes, then again open the bottom vent about $^1/_4$ inch (6 mm). Continue to grill, turning the loin every 15 minutes, until an instant-read thermometer registers 170°F (77°C), about 1$^1/_2$ hours longer. Transfer to a cutting board, cover loosely with aluminum foil, and let stand for 10–15 minutes before slicing.

Meanwhile, prepare the onion confit: Preheat an oven to 300°F (150°C). Place the butter on a large baking sheet and melt in the oven, 4–5 minutes. Remove and spread the onions on the baking sheet to make a layer about 1 inch (2.5 cm) deep. Add the bay leaves, thyme, savory, pepper, and salt. Drizzle evenly with the olive oil. Bake the onions, turning every 10–15 minutes, until light golden brown and reduced in volume by nearly half, about 1$^1/_2$ hours.

Thinly slice the pork. Spoon the onion confit onto individual plates and top with the pork. Serve hot or at room temperature.

Serves 10–12

$^1/_3$ cup ($^1/_3$ oz/10 g) fresh rosemary leaves, plus 12 fresh rosemary branches, each 14–16 inches (35–40 cm) long

$^1/_3$ cup ($^1/_3$ oz/10 g) chopped fresh sage

1 teaspoon coarse sea salt

6 peppercorns

2 tablespoons olive oil

1 boneless pork loin, 4 lb (2 kg)

FOR THE CONFIT:

$^1/_4$ cup (2 oz/60 g) unsalted butter, cut into pieces

4 lb (2 kg) red onions, thickly sliced

2 bay leaves

2 tablespoons fresh thyme leaves

1 tablespoon fresh winter savory leaves or $^1/_2$ teaspoon dried winter savory

1 teaspoon freshly ground pepper

$^1/_2$ teaspoon salt

$^1/_4$ cup (2 fl oz/60 ml) olive oil

Pork Loin with Orange-Ginger Glaze

Tiny, Mexican chiles and garlic infuse the meat overnight. You can roast potatoes and other root vegetables in the same pan, if you wish; cut them into 1½-inch (4-cm) pieces and add them one hour before the pork loin is done.

2 boneless pork loins, 3–3½ lb (1.5–1.75 kg) each, tied at 2-inch (5-cm) intervals

2 large cloves garlic, slivered

8–10 tiny red chiles, slivered

1 teaspoon coarse salt

½ teaspoon freshly ground pepper

¼ cup (2 fl oz/60 ml) olive oil

¼ cup (2 fl oz/60 ml) orange juice

FOR THE ORANGE-GINGER GLAZE:

2 cups (1¼ lb/625 g) orange marmalade

1 yellow onion, minced

2 slices fresh ginger, peeled and minced

1 small clove garlic, minced

½ cup (4 fl oz/125 ml) orange juice

2–3 tablespoons Grand Marnier or other orange liqueur

Zest strips from ½ orange

Using a small knife, make 20–24 small slits in each of the pork loins. Alternately tuck a garlic sliver into half of the slits and a chile sliver into the other half. Rub the meat with the salt and pepper. Set each pork loin in a large nonaluminum pan. In a bowl, whisk together the olive oil and orange juice; pour half over each loin. Cover and refrigerate for at least 4 hours. Bring to room temperature before roasting.

In a small, heavy saucepan over medium heat, stir together the orange marmalade, onion, ginger, and garlic, and bring to a boil. Stir in ¼ cup (2 fl oz/60 ml) orange juice, reduce the heat to low, and simmer for 5 minutes. Stir in 2 tablespoons of the Grand Marnier, taste, and adjust the flavorings. Remove from the heat and set aside.

Preheat the oven to 400°F (200°C). Remove the pork from the marinade and transfer to a large roasting pan. Pour the marinade into a small saucepan over high heat, bring to a boil, remove from the heat, and set aside. Place the roasting pan over high heat, and brown on all sides, about 5 minutes, and pour the hot marinade around the meat.

Roast the pork, basting with the orange-ginger glaze every 10 minutes, until the meat is browned, and glazed, or an instant-read thermometer registers 155°–160°F (68°–71°C), about 1½ hours. Transfer the meat to a cutting board, loosely tent with aluminum foil, and let rest for 15 minutes before carving.

Cut the pork across the grain into thin slices, arrange on a warmed platter, and garnish with the orange zest. Serve immediately.

Serves 10–12

Roast Pork Loin in Ginger Marinade

Serve this savory, Asian inspired pork loin on a bed of sautéed spinach with ginger and sesame oil, sprinkled with sesame seeds. A medium-bodied red wine is a perfect accompaniment. Any leftover pork makes great sandwiches.

In a food processor or blender, combine the green onions, ginger, garlic, chicken stock, soy sauce, tomato sauce or ketchup, brown sugar, and red pepper flakes. Purée to form a marinade. Place the pork loin in a nonaluminum container and pour the marinade over the top. Turn to coat well, then cover and refrigerate for at least 6 hours or for up to overnight. Bring the pork to room temperature before roasting.

Preheat the oven to 350°F (180°C).

Transfer the pork loin to a roasting pan. Reserve the marinade. Roast the pork, basting occasionally with the reserved marinade, until an instant-read thermometer inserted into the thickest part of the loin registers 147°–150°F (64°–65°C) or the meat is pale pink when cut in the thickest portion, about 1 hour. Stop basting at least 5 minutes before the pork is done; discard the remaining marinade.

Transfer the pork to a cutting board and cover loosely with aluminum foil. Let rest for 10 minutes.

Slice the pork thinly and arrange the slices on a warmed platter. Serve immediately.

Serves 4

3 green (spring) onions, including the tender green tops, chopped

1 piece fresh ginger, 3 inches (7.5 cm) long, peeled and sliced

2 cloves garlic

1/2 cup (4 fl oz/125 ml) Chicken Stock (page 288) or broth

3 tablespoons soy sauce

2 tablespoons tomato sauce or tomato ketchup

1/4 cup (2 oz/60 g) firmly packed brown sugar

Small pinch red pepper flakes

1 boneless pork loin, 2 1/2 lb (1.25 kg), trimmed of all fat

Spicy Grilled Ribs

For an all-American barbecue, serve Midwestern Coleslaw (page 285) and corn bread as side dishes. For a more Latin touch, prepare black beans and corn on the cob rubbed with chile powder and lime. In either case, a cold, crisp beer is an ideal accompaniment.

2 racks baby back ribs, about 4 lb (2 kg) total weight

2–3 tablespoons chili powder

¼ teaspoon *each* salt and freshly ground pepper

FOR THE SAUCE:

1 cup (8 fl oz/250 ml) tomato ketchup

⅓ cup (3 fl oz/80 ml) cider vinegar

¼ cup (2 fl oz/60 ml) orange juice

⅓ cup (3 oz/90 g) firmly packed brown sugar, or ½ cup (6 oz/185 g) honey

4 cloves garlic, minced

2 tablespoons Worcestershire sauce

2 tablespoons chili powder

1 tablespoon dry mustard

2 teaspoons ground cumin

½ teaspoon ground ginger

¼ teaspoon ground cinnamon

Preheat the oven to 350°F (180°C).

Rub the ribs evenly with the chili powder, salt, and pepper. Place on a rack in a roasting pan and cover loosely with aluminum foil. Bake until very tender, about 1 hour.

Meanwhile, make the sauce: In a saucepan, stir together the ketchup, vinegar, orange juice, brown sugar, garlic, Worcestershire sauce, chili powder, dry mustard, cumin, ginger, and cinnamon. Place over medium heat and bring to a simmer. Cook uncovered, stirring occasionally, until the flavors are well blended, about 15 minutes. Remove from the heat and set aside.

Prepare a hot fire for direct-heat cooking in a charcoal grill (see pages 8–9) or preheat a broiler (grill). If using a grill, position the rack 4–6 inches (10–15 cm) above the fire. Oil the grill rack.

Sprinkle the ribs lightly with salt and pepper and place on the oiled grill rack or on an oiled rack in a broiler pan. Brush liberally with some of the sauce. Grill or broil until caramelized, 8–10 minutes. Turn, brush with additional sauce, and cook on the second side until crusty and caramelized, about 8 minutes longer.

Transfer to a cutting board and cut the ribs apart. Arrange on a warmed platter and serve. Pour the remaining sauce into a small bowl and pass at the table.

Serves 4

Fish & Shellfish

Grilled Tuna with Sun-Dried Tomatoes and Olives

Tuna has a meaty texture that stands up well to the heat of the grill. Serve the tuna with roast potatoes and sautéed greens like Swiss chard or escarole (Batavian endive). Grilled eggplant (aubergine) and zucchini (courgettes) are also fine accompaniments.

1/4 cup (2 oz/60 g) finely chopped oil-packed sun-dried tomatoes

1/4 cup (1 1/4 oz/37 g) chopped pitted Gaeta or Niçoise olives

1/4 cup (1/3 oz/10 g) chopped fresh mint or thyme

2 teaspoons minced garlic

4 tablespoons (2 fl oz/60 ml) extra-virgin olive oil

3 tablespoons lemon juice

2 tablespoons oil from sun-dried tomatoes

1/2 teaspoon freshly ground pepper, plus more as needed

4 tuna fillets, 6–7 oz (185–220 g) each

Salt

Prepare a medium fire in a charcoal grill (see pages 8–9) or preheat a broiler (grill). If using a grill, position the grill rack 4–6 inches (10–15 cm) above the fire.

In a bowl, stir together the sun-dried tomatoes, olives, mint or thyme, garlic, 3 tablespoons of the olive oil, the lemon juice, oil from the tomatoes, and 1/2 teaspoon pepper. Set aside.

Brush the remaining 1 tablespoon olive oil evenly over both sides of the fish fillets. Sprinkle the fillets with salt and pepper.

Place the fish on the grill rack, or place on a rack in a broiler pan and place under the broiler. Grill or broil, turning once, until done to your liking, 3 minutes on each side for medium-rare.

Transfer the fish fillets to warmed individual plates and spoon an equal amount of the tomato-olive mixture over each serving. Serve immediately.

Serves 4

Fish with Olives, Pine Nuts, Basil, and Wine

This elegant, yet simple fish dish, redolent of the flavors of Italy, is best served with a chilled bottle of the same wine used in the cooking. Accompany it with roasted baby artichokes, or artichoke hearts.

Preheat the oven to 350°F (180°C). Spread the nuts on a baking sheet and toast in the oven until they take on color and are fragrant, 5–8 minutes. Remove from the oven and set aside. Raise the oven temperature to 400°F (200°C).

Sprinkle the fish fillets with salt and pepper. Place in a baking dish in which they fit in a single layer. In a small bowl, stir together 3 tablespoons of the olive oil and the wine. Pour over the fish fillets. Top with half of the garlic and half of the basil, and then distribute the olives around the fillets. Cover with aluminum foil.

Cook in the oven until the fish is opaque throughout when pierced with a knife, 10–15 minutes. The timing will depend upon the thickness of the fillets. Using a slotted spatula, transfer the fillets to warmed individual plates.

Pour the pan juices, olives, and reserved pine nuts into a small sauté pan over medium heat and swirl in the remaining 1 tablespoon olive oil and the remaining garlic and basil. When warm and fragrant, spoon over the fish. Serve immediately.

Serves 4

1/4 cup (1 oz/30 g) pine nuts

4 firm white fish fillets such as snapper, rock cod, flounder, sea bass, halibut, or swordfish, 6–7 oz (185–220 g) each

Kosher salt and freshly ground pepper

4 tablespoons (2 fl oz/60 ml) extra-virgin olive oil

1/3 cup (3 fl oz/80 ml) dry white wine

1 1/2 tablespoons finely minced garlic

5 tablespoons (1/3 oz/10 g) fresh basil leaves, shredded

1/2 cup (2 1/2 oz/75 g) Mediterranean-style green and/or black olives, pitted

Grilled Fish in a Spicy Citrus Marinade

Serve this light, zingy fish dish for weekend guests or as a weeknight supper. A plate of simple sautéed greens or a dish of black or red beans and rice will round out the menu perfectly.

4 firm, mild white fish fillets such as grouper, sea bass, flounder, cod, or halibut, about 6 oz (185 g) each

Sea salt or kosher salt

1 small yellow onion, diced

1 walnut-sized piece fresh ginger, peeled and thinly sliced

1 small bunch fresh cilantro (fresh coriander), chopped

1 tablespoon chopped garlic

2 teaspoons minced jalapeño chile

2 teaspoons grated lime zest

1 teaspoon freshly ground pepper

1/4 cup (2 fl oz/60 ml) lime juice

1/4 cup (2 fl oz/60 ml) olive oil

1 lime, quartered (optional)

Place the fish fillets in a nonaluminum container and sprinkle lightly with salt. In a food processor, combine the onion, ginger, cilantro, garlic, chile, lime zest, pepper, lime juice, and olive oil. Using on-off pulses, pulse until a paste forms. Rub the paste evenly over both sides of each fish fillet. Cover and marinate in the refrigerator for at least 2 hours or for up to 4 hours.

Prepare a medium fire for direct-heat cooking in a charcoal grill (see pages 8–9) or preheat a broiler (griller). If using a grill, position the grill rack 4–6 inches (10–15 cm) above the fire. Oil the grill rack.

Sprinkle the fish fillets with salt again. Place on the oiled grill rack or on an oiled rack on a broiler pan andplace under the broiler. Grill or broil, turning once, until opaque throughout when pierced with a knife, 3–4 minutes on each side.

Transfer to warmed individual plates. Serve immediately, with lime wedges for squeezing, if desired.

Serves 4

Niçoise Salad with Grilled Tuna

From Nice, on the French Riviera, comes this simply composed salad rich in the flavors of the land and the sea. The salad can be served at room temperature, making it an excellent candidate for enjoying outdoors.

In a saucepan, combine the potatoes with water to cover by 2–3 inches (5–7.5 cm) and $^1/_2$ teaspoon of the salt. Bring to a boil, reduce the heat to medium-low, and cook until tender, about 20 minutes. Drain, rinse with cold running water, and let stand until cool to the touch. Peel and cut into $^1/_2$-inch (12-mm) cubes. Set aside.

Next, bring a saucepan three-fourths full of water to a boil. Add $^1/_4$ teaspoon salt and the green beans. Cook until the beans are just tender, 5–7 minutes. Drain, rinse with cold running water until cool, and drain again. Set aside.

Prepare a hot fire for direct-heat cooking in a grill (see pages 8–9). Position the grill rack 4–6 inches (10–15 cm) above the fire.

Drain the anchovies well. Arrange the lettuces on a serving platter. Place the potatoes, green beans, tomatoes, cucumber, and eggs in separate piles on the lettuces. Drape the anchovy fillets on top.

To make the dressing, in a small bowl, combine the olive oil, vinegar, garlic, $^1/_2$ teaspoon salt, and the pepper; mix well. Pour the dressing over the salad.

Cut the tuna into 6 serving pieces. Rub on both sides with about $^1/_2$ teaspoon each salt and pepper. Place the tuna directly on the grill rack. Cook, turning once, until cooked to your liking when the center is pierced with a knife, 2–3 minutes on each side for rare or about 6 minutes on each side for well done.

Transfer the tuna to the platter. Top with the olives and capers (if using).

Serves 6

1 lb (500 g) boiling potatoes

1¼ teaspoons salt, plus more as needed

1 lb (500 g) young, thin green beans, trimmed

16 anchovy fillets in olive oil

2 cups (2 oz/60 g) mixed young lettuces

5 tomatoes, thinly sliced

1 cucumber, thinly sliced

4 hard-boiled eggs, peeled and thinly sliced

½ cup (4 fl oz/125 ml) extra-virgin olive oil

¼ cup (2 fl oz/60 ml) red wine vinegar

1 clove garlic, minced

½ teaspoon freshly ground pepper

1⅓ lb (655 g) tuna fillet, about ½ inch (12 mm) thick

½ cup (2½ oz/75 g) oil-packed black olives

1 tablespoon capers (optional)

Maple-Glazed Salmon Fillet with Oven-Roasted Sweet Potatoes

A whole salmon fillet basted with maple syrup quickly cooks to perfection in this simple but elegant recipe. The maple syrup begins to give a caramelized edge to the potatoes just as the salmon is done. If you like, garnish with snipped fresh chives.

Preheat the oven to 400°F (200°C).

In a bowl, toss the sweet potatoes with the melted butter, $1/2$ teaspoon salt, pepper to taste, and the cinnamon to coat evenly. Arrange in a single layer on a large baking sheet. Place in the oven and roast until the potatoes begin to brown on the bottom, about 20 minutes.

Meanwhile, in a small saucepan, stir together the maple syrup and Worcestershire sauce. Place over medium heat and bring to a boil. Reduce the heat to low and cook until thickened and reduced by one-half, about 5 minutes. Remove from the heat and set aside.

Run your fingers over the salmon fillet to detect any errant bones; remove and discard any you find. Sprinkle the salmon fillet with salt and pepper.

Remove the baking sheet from the oven. Raise the oven temperature to 450°F (230°C). Carefully turn over the sweet potatoes and place the salmon fillet on top of them. Brush half of the maple mixture evenly on the salmon fillet. Return the baking sheet to the oven and roast for 10 minutes. Remove from the oven and baste the salmon with the remaining maple syrup mixture. Return to the oven once again and roast until the flesh is opaque at the center when pierced with a knife at the thickest point, 5–10 minutes longer.

Divide the salmon into serving portions, and serve. Arrange on warmed individual plates with the sweet potatoes.

Serves 6

4 orange-fleshed sweet potatoes, about 2 lb (1 kg) total weight, peeled and thinly sliced on the diagonal

2 tablespoons unsalted butter, melted

$1/2$ teaspoon salt, plus more if needed

Freshly ground pepper

Pinch of ground cinnamon

$1/3$ cup (3 fl oz/80 ml) pure maple syrup

2 tablespoons Worcestershire sauce

1 whole skinless salmon fillet, about $1^2/3$ lb (815 g)

Saffron-Scented Halibut with Spinach, Zucchini, and Tomato

1 lemon

3 tablespoons olive oil

Pinch of saffron threads

6 halibut fillets, each 6–7 oz (185–220 g) and about 3/4 inch (2 cm) thick, skinned

Coarse salt and freshly ground pepper

FOR THE VEGETABLES:

3 tablespoons olive oil

3 large shallots, diced

1/8 teaspoon saffron threads

1 lb (500 g) spinach, tough stems removed

Coarse salt and freshly ground pepper

3 or 4 small zucchini (courgettes), diced

2 large tomatoes, peeled, seeded, and diced

Juice of 1 lemon

1/2 bunch fresh flat-leaf (Italian) parsley, minced

In a small bowl, whisk together the juice of the lemon, the olive oil, and the saffron. Season the fish fillets with coarse salt and pepper. Place in a nonaluminum dish in a single layer. Pour the oil mixture over the fish and turn to coat. Cover and refrigerate for 1–2 hours.

Preheat the oven to 450°F (230°C).

Spray a roasting pan with nonstick cooking spray and place in the oven until hot, about 5 minutes. Sprinkle a little coarse salt in the hot pan. Lift the fish fillets from the marinade, reserving the marinade, and place them, skin sides down, in the hot pan. Roast until opaque throughout when pierced with a knife, 7–10 minutes.

Meanwhile, prepare the vegetables: In a large nonaluminum sauté pan over medium-high heat, warm the olive oil. Add the shallots and sauté until they begin to soften, 2–3 minutes. Add the saffron and cook until the shallots are soft, about 4 minutes longer. Transfer 1 tablespoon of the shallots to a small dish and set aside.

Raise the heat under the sauté pan to high. Working in 3 batches, add the spinach leaves to the shallots remaining in the pan. Sauté, tossing constantly, until the spinach is wilted but still bright green, 4–5 minutes. Transfer to a plate, season with salt and pepper, and keep warm. Place the sauté pan over medium heat and add the reserved shallots. Add the zucchini and cook, stirring occasionally, until it begins to soften, 2–3 minutes. Add the tomatoes and cook, stirring, until the tomatoes begin to soften, 3–4 minutes. Add the reserved marinade, raise the heat to high, and cook until the sauce is slightly thickened and the vegetables are just tender, 5–7 minutes longer. Season with salt, pepper, and lemon juice.

Divide the spinach among each individual plate. Top with a fish fillet, and spoon the zucchini mixture over the fish. Sprinkle the plate with the parsley and serve.

Serves 6

Sea Bass with Olive Vinaigrette

A well-seasoned vinaigrette enhanced with olives, capers, and herbs makes a quick sauce for baked fish. You will have roasted bell pepper left over; if desired, slice it and add to a salad, or reserve it for a sandwich the following day.

To make the vinaigrette, preheat a broiler (grill). Cut the bell peppers in half lengthwise and remove the stem, seeds, and ribs. Place the peppers, cut sides down, on a baking sheet. Broil (grill) until the skins blacken and blister. Remove from the broiler, drape the bell peppers loosely with aluminum foil, and let cool for 10 minutes, and then peel away the skin. Finely dice three-quarters of the bell peppers. Reserve the remaining one-fourth of the pepper for another use (see note).

In a small bowl, whisk together the diced bell pepper, black and green olives, garlic, parsley, capers, extra-virgin olive oil, and lemon juice. Season with salt and pepper. Set aside.

Preheat the oven to 375°F (190°C).

Put the 1 1/2 teaspoon olive oil in a small baking dish. Add the sea bass and turn to coat. Season with salt and pepper. Spoon the wine around the fish. Bake until the fish is opaque throughout and just flakes with a fork, 12–15 minutes.

Using a spatula, transfer the fish to a warmed dinner plate. Top with the olive vinaigrette and serve.

Serves 4

FOR THE OLIVE VINAIGRETTE:

2 red bell peppesr (capsicums)

1/4 cup black olives, pitted and chopped

1/4 cup green olives, pitted and chopped

3 small cloves garlic, minced

3 tablespoons minced fresh parsley

1 tablespoon capers, chopped

3 tablespoons extra-virgin olive oils

1 teaspoon lemon juice

Salt and freshly ground pepper

1 1/2 tablespoons olive oil

4 skinless sea bass fillets, each about 6 oz (185 g)

Salt and freshly ground pepper

1/4 cup dry white wine

Trout Wrapped in Grape Leaves
with Lemon-Basil Mayonnaise Sauce

Wrapping fish in fresh grape leaves for grilling protects the fish from the direct heat of the coals and imparts a subtle flavor. If fresh leaves are unavailable, substitute leaves packed in brine and rinse well before using.

FOR THE MAYONNAISE SAUCE:

¼ cup (¼ oz/7 g) fresh basil leaves

1 cup (8 fl oz/250 ml) mayonnaise

¼ cup (2 fl oz/60 ml) lemon juice

1 tablespoon olive oil

½ teaspoon freshly ground pepper

¼ teaspoon salt

4 whole trout, about 10 oz (315 g) each

2 lemons, halved, plus 4 slices for garnish (optional)

½ teaspoon salt

½ teaspoon freshly ground pepper

8 long fresh thyme sprigs

16–24 large fresh grape leaves

4 fresh basil sprigs (optional)

Prepare a medium-hot fire for direct-heat cooking in a grill (see pages 8–9). Position the grill rack 4–6 inches (10–15 cm) above the fire.

To make the sauce, chop the basil and put in a small bowl. Add the mayonnaise, lemon juice, olive oil, pepper, and salt and stir until thoroughly mixed. Taste and adjust the seasonings. Cover and refrigerate until ready to serve.

Rub the cavities and outside skin of the trout with the lemon halves, squeezing a little juice on them as you do so. Sprinkle inside and out with the salt and pepper, then tuck 2 thyme sprigs inside each cavity. Lay 1 grape leaf on a work surface and place 1 fish on top. Wrap the leaf around the fish. Repeat with more leaves until the fish is snugly wrapped in two layers of leaves. Wrap all the fish in the same manner. Fasten the leaves with toothpicks or skewers, if necessary.

Place the wrapped trout, seam side down, directly on the grill rack or in a grill basket directly on the grill. Grill until the grape leaves are slightly browned on the first side, about 5 minutes. Turn and cook until browned on the second side, 4–5 minutes longer. Remove some of the grape leaves from 1 trout and test the flesh with a fork; it should just flake easily.

To serve, place the trout on 4 individual plates and let diners unwrap their own fish; provide a plate for the discarded grape leaves. (Alternatively, remove the grape leaves yourself and place the fish on individual plates.) Garnish each plate with a lemon slice and a basil sprig, if desired. Serve, passing the sauce at the table.

Serves 4

Monkfish with Chipotle Sauce

Chipotle chiles are often sold canned in adobo sauce in Latin American markets and specialty-food stores. This recipe calls for monkfish, but any full-flavored fish that can stand up to the spicy sauce will work well.

FOR THE CHIPOTLE SAUCE:

1 tablespoon olive oil

2 cloves garlic

1 canned chipotle chile in adobo sauce

1/4 cup (1 1/2 oz/45 g) jarred chopped roasted red pepper

2/3 cup (5 fl oz/150 ml) mayonnaise

3 tablespoons sour cream

3 tablespoons milk, or as needed

1 teaspoon lime juice

1/4 teaspoon salt

2 tablespoons olive oil

2 tablespoons lime juice

2 teaspoons Hungarian sweet paprika

1/2 teaspoon salt

1/4 teaspoon freshlyground pepper

2 1/2–3 lb (1.25–1.5 kg) monkfish fillets, about 1 inch (2.5 cm) thick

To make the sauce, in a small saucepan over low heat, warm the olive oil for 1 minute. Add the garlic cloves, cover tightly, and cook, stirring occasionally, until lightly golden and soft, about 20 minutes. Remove from the heat and let cool.

In a food processor, combine the cooked garlic and oil, chipotle chile, red pepper, and 1/3 cup (2 1/2 fl oz/75 ml) of the mayonnaise. Process until smooth. Add the remaining 1/3 cup (2 1/2 fl oz/75 ml) mayonnaise, the sour cream, milk, lime juice, and salt. Process until smooth, adding another tablespoon or so of milk if needed to achieve a light and creamy sauce. Transfer to a bowl, cover, and refrigerate until serving.

In a small bowl, whisk together the olive oil, lime juice, paprika, salt, and pepper. Place the monkfish pieces in a shallow nonaluminum dish and spoon the olive oil mixture over the top. Turn the fish to coat. Cover and refrigerate for 45 minutes. Remove from the refrigerator 15 minutes before grilling.

Prepare a hot fire for direct-heat cooking in a grill (see pages 8–9). Position the grill rack 4–6 inches (10–15 cm) above the fire.

If the monkfish is in large pieces, place them directly on the grill rack. If the monkfish is in small pieces, place them in 1 or more lightly oiled hinged grill baskets. Cook, turning once, until the fish is opaque throughout when pierced with a knife, and firm to the touch, 4–5 minutes on each side.

Transfer the fish fillets to a warmed platter and serve, passing the sauce at the table.

Serves 6

Tangy Salmon Steaks

A pinch of ground cloves brings out the full flavor of the sweet, mustardy marinade. Serve with Butter Roasted Corn on the Cob (page 237) and sliced cherry or grape tomatoes, and a green salad.

In a small bowl, stir together the mustard, soy sauce, brown sugar, garlic, and cloves. Spread half the mixture over the bottom of a shallow nonaluminum dish just large enough to hold the salmon steaks snugly.

Pat the salmon steaks dry with paper towels and place in the dish. Spread the remaining mustard mixture over the salmon, cover, and refrigerate for 45 minutes. Remove from the refrigerator 15 minutes before grilling.

Prepare a hot fire for direct-heat cooking in a grill (sees page 8–9). Position the grill rack 4–6 inches (10–15 cm) above the fire.

Place the fish steaks on the grill rack. Cook, turning once, until the fish is opaque throughout when pierced with a knife and firm to the touch, 4–5 minutes on each side.

Transfer to warmed individual plates and serve immediately.

Serves 4

¼ cup (2 oz/60 g) Dijon mustard

¼ cup (2 fl oz/60 ml) soy sauce

2 tablespoons dark brown sugar

1 small clove garlic, minced

Pinch of ground cloves

4 salmon steaks, each about 10 oz (315 g) and 1 inch (2.5 cm) thick

Mixed Seafood Grill

Place the clams and mussels in separate large bowls and add cold water to cover. Stir 1 tablespoon cornstarch into each bowl. Let stand for 30 minutes, then drain and rinse under running cold water. Place the clams and mussels in separate pots of cold water and set aside.

Meanwhile, place the shrimp in a large bowl and drizzle with the olive oil. Sprinkle with the basil and chives. Mix well, cover, and refrigerate for 45 minutes.

In a small bowl, mix together the butter, paprika, salt, and pepper. Rub this mixture over both sides of the fish fillets and place in a shallow nonaluminum dish. Cover and refrigerate for 30 minutes. Remove the shrimp and the fish from the refrigerator 15 minutes before grilling. Thread the shrimp onto metal skewers.

Prepare a hot fire for direct-heat cooking in a covered grill (see pages 8–9). Position the grill rack 4–6 inches (10–15 cm) above the fire.

Preheat the oven to 250°F (120°C). Drain the mussels and clams, discarding any that do not close to the touch. Place the mussels in a lightly oiled hinged grill basket. Place the clams around the edges of the rack and place on the grill. Cover the grill, and cook for 5 minutes. Place the basket holding the mussels on the center of the rack, cover, and continue to cook until both the clams and mussels have opened, about 8 minutes longer. Transfer to a large, shallow heatproof serving dish, discarding any that have not opened, and keep warm in the oven.

Lightly oil the hinged grill basket and place the fish fillets in it. Set on the grill rack along with the skewered shrimp. Cook uncovered, turning once, until the shrimp have turned pink and the fish fillets are opaque throughout when pierced with a knife, about 3 minutes on each side.

Transfer the fish and shrimp to the dish holding the clams and mussels. Garnish with the lemon wedges and parsley and serve. *Serves 6*

24 steamer clams, well scrubbed

24 mussels, well scrubbed and debearded

2 tablespoons cornstarch (cornflour)

24 large shrimp (prawns), peeled and deveined

2 tablespoons olive oil

2 teaspoons minced fresh basil

2 teaspoons snipped fresh chives

2 tablespoons unsalted butter, at room temperature

4 teaspoons Hungarian hot paprika

1/2 teaspoon salt

1/2 teaspoon freshly ground pepper

1 1/2 (750 g) firm fish fillets such as weakfish, haddock, snapper, or pompano, about 1/2 inch (12 mm) thick

2 large lemons, cut into wedges

Fresh parsley sprigs

Roasted Fish Fillets with Tomato Salsa

The juices from the tomato salsa mingle with the fish as it roasts to create an exquisite Mediterranean-style main course, ideal for late summer when good tomatoes are plentiful. Serve with rustic bread for mopping up the flavorful juices.

Leaves from 1 bunch fresh flat-leaf (Italian) parsley, finely chopped

14 large fresh basil leaves, finely chopped

Leaves from 5 fresh oregano sprigs, finely chopped

4 large Vidalia onions, chopped

10 oil-packed sun-dried tomato halves, drained and minced

3 large, firm ripe tomatoes, peeled, seeded and minced

1/4 cup (2 oz/60 g) small capers

1 teaspoon red pepper flakes

Coarse salt and freshly ground black pepper

About 3 tablespoons extra-virgin olive oil

2 sea bass or red snapper fillets with skin intact, about 1 1/4 lb (625 g) each

Juice of 1/2 lemon

About 1 tablespoon olive oil

In a bowl, combine the chopped parsely, three-fourths of the chopped basil, three-fourths of the chopped oregano, one-fourth of the chopped onion, the sun dried tomatoes, fresh tomatoes, capers, and red pepper flakes; mix well. Season with salt and pepper, then add 2 tablespoons of the olive oil or enough to bind the salsa lightly. Taste and adjust the seasonings. Set aside.

Preheat the oven to 425°F (220°C). Lightly oil a baking dish large enough to hold the fillets in a single layer.

Scatter the remaining onions in the bottom of the dish. Rinse the fish fillets, pat dry with paper towels, and place, skin sides down, directly on the onions. Season to taste with salt and pepper. Sprinkle the fillets with the remaining basil and oregano, and then drizzle with the lemon juice and 1 tablespoon olive oil.

Roast until the fish is half-cooked, 10–11 minutes. Spoon 3–4 tablespoons of the salsa with its juices directly over the fillets. Return the fillets to the oven and continue to roast until the fish is opaque throughout when pierced with a knife, 9–10 minutes longer.

Transfer the remaining salsa to a small serving bowl. Serve the fish directly from the baking dish. Pass the salsa at the table.

Serves 6

Grilled Tuna, White Bean, and Arugula Salad

This main-course salad, dressed with a lemon-garlic vinaigrette, is the perfect luncheon centerpiece for your just-arrived summertime guests. The fish can also be cooked in a broiler (grill) using the same timing.

Cut away the tough core portion of the fennel and dice. Place in a large nonaluminum bowl. Add the beans, tomatoes, onion, and olives and mix well.

In a small bowl, whisk together the lemon juice, garlic, thyme, 1 teaspoon salt, and the $^{1}/_{4}$ teaspoon pepper. Whisk in the olive oil. Remove and reserve $^{1}/_{4}$ cup (2 fl oz/60 ml) of the lemon dressing. Add the remaining oil mixture to the bean mixture, toss well, and marinate for at least 2 hours or for up to 4 hours.

About 45 minutes before serving, place the tuna in a shallow glass dish. Add the soy sauce to the reserved lemon dressing, and pour over the tuna. Cover and let stand at cool room temperature.

Prepare a medium-hot fire for direct-heat cooking in a charcoal grill (see pages 8–9). Position the grill rack 4–5 inches (10–13 cm) above the fire. Oil the grill rack. When the coals are ready, remove the tuna from the marinade and place on the oiled grill. Grill, turning once, until seared on the outside but still pink in the center, 1$^{1}/_{2}$ minutes on each side, or until done to your liking. Remove from the grill rack and sprinkle lightly with salt and pepper. Cut into slices about $^{1}/_{4}$ inch (6mm) thick.

Meanwhile, reserve one-third of the arugula and set aside. Roughly chop the remaining arugula and add to the bean mixture. Mix well. Taste and adjust the seasonings. To serve, arrange one-sixth of the reserved arugula on one side of each individual plate. Mound one-sixth of the salad in the center of each plate and arrange the tuna on top, dividing evenly. Sprinkle the tuna with the lemon zest. Serve immediately.

Serves 6

1 fennel bulb, trimmed and quartered

3 cans (15 oz/470 g each) cannellini beans, rinsed, drained, and patted dry

6 plum tomatoes, halved seeded, and diced

1 cup (4 oz/125 g) chopped red onion

15 Kalamata olives, pitted and slivered

$^{1}/_{4}$ cup (2 fl oz/60 ml) lempn juice

2 teaspoons finely chopped garlic

1$^{1}/_{2}$ teaspoons minced fresh thyme

1 teaspoon salt, plus more as needed

$^{1}/_{4}$ teaspoon freshly ground pepper, plus more if needed

$^{3}/_{4}$ cup (6 fl/180 ml) olive oil

1$^{1}/_{2}$ lb (750 g) tuna fillet

2 teaspoons soy sauce

$^{1}/_{2}$ lb (250 g) arugula (rocket)

2 teaspoons grated lemon zest

Cloaked Fish Stuffed with Bok Choy

Red snapper, black sea bass, trout, tilapia, and whiting are excellent candidates for
this unusual recipe, which balances the slight bitterness of the bok choy with the mild
flavor of the fresh fish. Ask your fishmonger to bone the whole fish.

2 tablespoons, plus 2
teaspoons olive oil

1 small clove garlic, minced

1/2 teaspoon peeled and
minced fresh ginger

1 large fresh shiitake
mushroom cap, sliced

1/3 cup (about 2 oz/60 g)
chopped prosciutto

1 1/2 lb (750 g) bok choy, leaves
separated, stems removed and
roughly chopped

1 small carrot, peeled and
grated

1/4 cup (2 fl oz/60 ml) plus
1 tablespoon Chicken Stock
(page 288), or broth

1 tablespoon soy sauce

1 tablespoon cornstarch
(cornflour)

4 whole fish, about 1 1/3 lb
(655 g) each, boned (see note)

Salt and freshly ground pepper

8 or more large butter (Boston)
or iceberg lettuce leaves

In a frying pan over medium heat, warm 2 tablespoons of the olive oil. Add the
garlic and ginger and cook until fragrant, about 1 minute. Add the mushroom,
prosciutto, bok choy stems, carrot, the 1/4 cup (2 fl oz/60 ml) chicken stock. Cook
until the bok choy stems are tender, 3–4 minutes. Add the bok choy leaves and the
soy sauce and cook until the leaves wilt, about 30 seconds. Reduce the heat to low.

In a small bowl, whisk the cornstarch with the remaining 1 tablespoon chicken
stock. Stir into the bok choy mixture and cook, stirring constantly, until the sauce
is thickened, about 30 seconds. Remove from the heat and let cool.

Prepare a hot fire for direct-heat cooking in a covered grill (see pages 8–9). Position
the grill rack 4–6 inches (10–15 cm) above the fire. Soak about 6 feet (2 m) kitchen
string in water to cover for at least 15 minutes.

Sprinkle the fish with salt and pepper. Working with 1 fish at a time, place it on
2 lettuce leaves, slightly overlapping, on a work surface. Spoon one-fourth of the
bok choy mixture into the fish cavity. Fold the leaves tightly over the fish and
secure the leaves in place by tying with kitchen string. Place the fish in a lightly
oiled hinged grill basket. Brush the fish with the 2 teaspoons olive oil.

Place the fish on the grill rack. Cover the grill and open the vents. Cook until the
lettuce is well browned on the underside, 5–7 minutes. Turn and continue to cook
until the fish is opaque throughout when pierced with a knife, 5–7 minutes longer.

Transfer the fish to warmed plates and serve. Let diners discard the leaves.

Serves 4

Skewers of Swordfish, Red Peppers, and Oranges

Serve these colorful skewers for an outdoor summer buffet, or as the light main dish for a casual weeknight. Accompany them with steamed basmati rice or couscous and sautéed fennel or zucchini (courgettes).

Grate the zest from 2 of the oranges, then juicethe zest oranges. Place the zest and juice in a small bowl and add the olive oil, vinegar, $1/4$ teaspoon salt, $1/8$ teaspoon of the pepper, and 3 tablespoons of the basil. Whisk well and pour over the swordfish in a nonaluminum dish. Turn the fish to coat evenly, cover with plastic wrap, and refrigerate, turning several times, for $1^1/2$–2 hours.

Cut 2 of the remaining oranges lengthwise into 8 neat wedges each. Cut each wedge in half crosswise and set aside. Grate enough zest from the remaining orange to measure 2 teaspoons and place the zest in a small bowl. Juice the zested orange and add 1 tablespoon of the juice to the bowl; reserve the remaining juice. Add to the bowl the remaining 3 tablespoons basil, $1/8$ teaspoon each salt and pepper, and the butter and mix well. Cover and marinate the fish at room temperature. At the same time, soak 4 wooden skewers in water to cover for 30 minutes.

Prepare a medium-hot fire for direct-heat cooking in a charcoal grill (see pages 8–9). Position the grill rack 4–6 inches (10–15 cm) above the fire. Oil the grill rack. Thread the bell pepper squares onto the skewers alternately with the orange wedges and swordfish cubes. Place the skewers on a rimmed baking sheet.

Place the skewers on the oiled grill rack. Grill, turning once and basting with the seasoned butter, until the fish is opaque throughout, 4–5 minutes on each side.

Transfer the skewers to a platter and season with salt. Drizzle the reserved orange juice over the top as desired, garnish with basil sprigs, and serve.

Serves 4

$1^1/3$ lb (21 oz/655 g) swordfish steaks, about 1 inch (2.5 cm) thick, boned, skinned, and cut into 1-inch (2.5-cm) cubes

5 thick-skinned navel oranges

$1/4$ cup (2 fl oz/60 ml) olive oil

1 tablespoon white balsamic vinegar or white wine vinegar

$1/4$ teaspoon plus $1/8$ teaspoon salt, plus more as needed

$1/4$ teaspoon freshly ground pepper

6 tablespoons ($1/2$ oz/15 g) julienned fresh basil leaves, plus several sprigs for garnish

$1/4$ cup (2 oz/60 g) unsalted butter, at room temperature

2 red bell peppers (capsicums), seeded and cut into 1-inch (2.5-cm) squares

Broiled Snapper on Toasted Sourdough

Toasted bread spread with a tangy mayonnaise-and-mustard sauce laced with pickles and onions pairs perfectly with the broiled fish in this tasty sandwich. For an easy meal, have your guests create their own sandwiches with the ingredients provided.

FOR THE TARTAR SAUCE:

3/4 cup (6 fl oz/180 ml) mayonnaise

1 1/2 tablespoons Dijon mustard

1 1/2 tablespoons minced yellow onion

1 1/2 tablespoons minced sweet pickle

1 1/2 teaspoons pickle juice

1 teaspoon lemon juice

1/2 teaspoon freshly ground pepper

1 lb (500 g) red or other snapper fillet, about 1/2 inch (12 mm) thick

2 tablespoons unsalted butter, melted

1 teaspoon freshly ground pepper

1/2 teaspoon salt

1 lemon, halved

4 sourdough rolls, split and toasted, or 8 slices sourdough bread, toasted

8 red lettuce leaves

Preheat a broiler (grill).

To make the tartar sauce, in a bowl, combine the mayonnaise, mustard, onion, pickle, pickle juice, lemon juice, and pepper. Stir until blended. Cover and refrigerate until ready to serve.

Cut the snapper fillet into 4 equal pieces. Brush each fillet on both sides with the melted butter. Sprinkle on both sides with the pepper and salt. Place the fillets on a broiler pan and place under the broiler about 6 inches (15 cm) from the heat source. Broil (grill), turning once, just until the flesh flakes easily with a fork, 3–4 minutes on each side. Do not overcook.

Remove from the broiler and squeeze the juice from the lemon halves evenly over the fillets. Spread the cut sides of the rolls or the 8 bread slices with some of the tartar sauce. Top the bottom halves of the rolls or one side of the 4 of the bread slices with the hot fish and lettuce leaves, dividing evenly. Top with the remaining roll halves or bread slices. Serve on individual plates.

Serves 4

Honey and Jalapeño Grilled Salmon

The sweetness of the honey, the spiciness of jalapeño chiles, and the tartness of the lime juice complement salmon deliciously. Serve with a pitcher of ice-cold margaritas for a festive South of the border–inspired evening.

Run your fingers carefully over the fillets to detect and remove any errant bones. Place the fish in a shallow nonaluminum dish. In a small bowl, stir together the lime juice, olive oil, 2 teaspoons of the minced jalapeno, the garlic, and lime zest. Pour mixture over the salmon and turn to coat well. Cover with the plastic wrap and refrigerate for 2 hours, turning occasionally. Bring to room temperature 30 minutes before cooking.

Prepare a medium-hot fire for direct-heat cooking in a charcoal grill (see pages 8–9). Position the grill rack 4–6 inches (10–15 cm) above the fire. Oil the grill rack.

Remove the salmon from the marinade, and pour the marinade into a small saucepan. Place the pan over high heat, bring to a boil, and boil until reduced by half. Stir in the honey and set aside to use as a glaze.

Place the salmon, flesh side down, on the oiled grill rack and grill, turning once, until the fish is opaque throughout when pierced with a knife, 6–7 minutes on each side. While the salmon is cooking, remove the zest from the 2 limes in long, narrow strips, then cut the limes in half.

When the salmon is done, transfer to a serving platter. Season each fillet with salt and squeeze some lime juice from the halved limes over each. Brush each fillet generously with the glaze, and sprinkle the lime zest and the remaining 2–3 teaspoons jalapeño evenly over the salmon. Serve immediately.

Serves 6

6 salmon fillets with skin intact, 6–7 oz (185–220 g) each

1/2 cup (4 fl oz/125 ml) lime juice

3 tablespoons olive oil

4–5 teaspoons minced jalapeño chile

1 teaspoon grated lime zest

1/4 cup (3 oz/90 g) honey

2 limes

Salt

Roasted Salmon Fillets on Leeks and Fennel

In this fast and easy main course, the sweet licorice flavor of the fennel and the subtle oniony quality of the leeks marry well with the rich salmon. This recipe is elegant enough for a formal dinner and can be increased to serve additional guests.

3 fennel bulbs

4 or 5 large leeks, including 1 inch (2.5 cm) of the green tops, julienned

Coarse salt and ground pepper

6 salmon fillets, 6–7 oz (185–220 g) each, skinned, erant bones removed

1 teaspoon fresh thyme leaves

Juice of 1 lemon

2–3 tablespoons extra-virgin olive oil

Preheat the oven to 425°F (220°C). Lightly oil a rimmed baking sheet with olive oil.

Cut off the stems and feathery tops and any bruised outer stalks from the fennel bulbs. Finely chop the tops of 1 bulb and reserve the tops of 1 of the other bulbs for garnish. Discard the remaining tops and any stems. Cut each bulb in half lengthwise and trim away the tough core. Cut the bulbs crosswise into thin slices.

Scatter about one-half of the leeks and about one-half of the sliced fennel bulbs evenly over the bottom of the prepared baking sheet. Lightly season with salt and pepper. Place the salmon fillets, skin sides down, on top of the vegetables. Season with salt, pepper, half of the thyme, and about $1/4$ cup ($1/3$ oz/10 g) of the chopped fennel tops. Drizzle with half of the lemon juice and half of the olive oil.

Roast the salmon until opaque throughout when pierced with a knife, about 20 minutes. The cooking time will depend upon the thickness of the fish; allow about 10 minutes for each inch (2.5 cm).

Meanwhile, place the remaining chopped leeks and fennel in a baking dish. Season the vegetables with salt and pepper and the remaining thyme, chopped fennel tops, lemon juice, and olive oil. Roast the vegetables alongside the fish until the vegetables are lightly browned and tender, about 15 minutes.

Using a spatula, transfer the salmon and vegetables to a warmed platter. Garnish with the reserved feathery fennel tops. Transfer the separately roasted vegetables to a warmed serving dish. Serve the fish and vegetables immediately.

Serves 6

Striped Bass Grilled in Banana Leaves

In a blender, combine the garlic, ginger, cilantro roots or stems, salt, and peppercorns. Blend until a smooth paste forms. Stir in the soy sauce. Set aside.

Rinse the fish under cold running water and pat dry with paper towels. Make 3 diagonal slashes, about 2 inches (5 cm) apart, almost to the bone across both sides of each fish. Sprinkle inside and out with salt and pepper. Stuff the cavities with the lemongrass, dividing evenly, and rub the spice paste inside and outside of both fish.

Bring a pot three-fourths full of water to a boil. Dip each banana leaf into the water until softened, about 4 seconds. Wipe dry. Set the leaves, glossy sides down, on a work surface and brush the centers with the oil. Place 1 fish in the center of each banana leaf. Fold the long sides up and over the fish so they overlap in the middle and secure with toothpicks. Fold the ends over to enclose the sides and thread in toothpicks to make a neat packet. If the leaves tear, wrap with extra leaves.

Prepare a hot fire for direct-heat cooking in a grill (see pages 8–9). Position the grill rack 4–6 inches (10–13 cm) above the fire. Meanwhile, in a saucepan over medium-high heat, combine the chiles, garlic, shallot, stock, sugar, and 1/4 teaspoon salt and bring to a boil. Reduce the heat to low, stir to combine, and simmer, uncovered, until reduced to a light syrup, about 3 minutes. Let cool and mix in the lime juice and cilantro to make the dipping sauce. Transfer to a bowl.

Place the fish packets on the grill rack and grill, turning every 3–4 minutes, for about 15 minutes. The fish should sizzle constantly while cooking. To check for doneness, carefully remove a fish packet from the grill. Using scissors, snip the banana leaf lengthwise along the center to open the packet. The fish should be opaque throughout when pierced with a knife; if not, rewrap and continue cooking. Serve hot, passing the dipping sauce.

Serves 4

6 large cloves garlic, halved

1 piece fresh ginger, 1 inch (2.5 cm), peeled

3 tablespoons fresh cilantro (fresh coriander) roots or stems

3/4 teaspoon *each* salt and whole cracked peppercorns

1 1/2 tablespoons Chinese light soy sauce

2 whole striped bass or red snapper, about 1 1/2 lb (750 g) each, heads and tails intact

Salt and freshly ground pepper

2 stalks lemongrass, trimmed, crushed, and cut into 2-inch (5-cm) lengths

2 large banana leaves, or more if needed

1 tablespoon vegetable oil

4 green serrano chiles, chopped

3 cloves garlic, chopped

1 shallot, chopped

1/3 cup (3 fl oz/80 ml) Chicken Stock (page 288), or broth

1 tablespoon sugar

Juice of 2 limes

2 tablespoons chopped fresh cilantro (fresh coriander)

Roast Fish in Moroccan Marinade

North African spices in the marinade infuse the fish with rich, aromatic flavors. Because of the intensity of the cooked spices, serve with a mild dish like couscous and grilled eggplant (aubergine) and roasted bell peppers (capsicums).

1 small yellow onion, grated

¼ cup (⅓ oz/10 g) chopped fresh flat-leaf (Italian) parsley

¼ cup (⅓ oz/10 g) chopped fresh cilantro (fresh coriander)

¼ cup (⅓ oz/10 g) chopped fresh mint

1 tablespoon minced garlic

1 tablespoon ground cumin

½ teaspoon cayenne pepper

⅓ cup (3 fl oz/80 ml) extra-virgin olive oil

¼ cup (2 fl oz/60 ml) lemon juice

4 firm white fish fillets such as cod, snapper, flounder, swordfish, or sea bass, about 6 oz (185 g) each

Salt and freshly ground black pepper

In a bowl, whisk together the onion, parsley, cilantro, mint, garlic, cumin, cayenne pepper, olive oil, and lemon juice to form a marinade. One at a time, dip the fish fillets in the marinade, coating well. Place in a nonaluminum container. Cover and marinate in the refrigerator for at least 2 hours or for up to 4 hours.

Preheat the oven to 450°F (230°C).

Transfer the fish fillets to a baking dish. Sprinkle with salt and black pepper. Cover with the marinade. Roast until the fish is opaque throughout when pierced with a knife, 10–15 minutes. The timing will depend upon the thickness of the fillets.

Transfer to warmed individual plates and serve immediately.

Serves 4

Roast Salmon with Melting Onions

Richly textured salmon, sweet and tender onions, crunchy almonds and crisp bread crumbs work beautifully together. Wlited spinach, sautéed fennel, or steamed broccoli makes an ideal accompaniment.

Preheat the oven to 350°F (180°C).

To make the nutty bread crumbs, place the bread cubes in a food processor. Pulse until coarse crumbs form. Spread the crumbs on a baking sheet. In a small bowl, stir the salt and pepper into the oil or butter and drizzle evenly over the bread crumbs. Bake, stirring occasionally to ensure even browning, until golden but not hard, 15–20 minutes. Remove from the oven and pour into a bowl. Spread the almonds on the same baking sheet and toast in the oven until they take on color and are fragrant, 5–8 minutes. Add to the crumbs and toss to mix. Set aside.

Raise the oven temperature to 450°F (230°C).

Meanwhile, in a sauté pan over medium heat, melt 4 tablespoons (2 oz/60 g) of the butter. Add the onions and cook, stirring occasionally, until tender and sweet, 15–20 minutes. Add the sage and lemon zest. Season with salt and pepper. Stir well. Remove from the heat and set aside.

Select a baking dish large enough to hold the salmon fillets. Butter the dish with the remaining 1 tablespoon of butter and place the fillets in the dish. Sprinkle with salt and pepper. Top with the onion mixture, covering evenly, then top with the nutty bread crumbs.

Bake until opaque throughout when pierced with a knife, 8–10 minutes. Transfer the fillets to warmed individual plates and serve immediately with the lemon wedges.

Serves 4

FOR THE NUTTY BREAD CRUMBS:

2 cups (4 oz/125 g) cubed Italian or French bread, without crusts

1 teaspoon salt

1 teaspoon freshly ground pepper

1/2 cup (4 fl oz/125 ml) olive oil or melted unsalted butter

1 cup (4 oz/125 g) sliced (flaked) almonds

5 tablespoons (2 1/2 oz/75 g) unsalted butter

2 yellow onions, cut into slices 1/4 inch (6 mm) thick

1 tablespoon chopped fresh sage

1 tablespoon grated lemon zest

Salt and freshly ground pepper

4 salmon fillets, about 6 oz (185 g) each, errant bones removed

1 lemon, quartered

Miso-Glazed Sea Bass

Miso, a staple of Japanese cooking, adds great flavor to marinades. Combined with mirin and sake—Japanese wines made from rice—and mixed with fresh ginger, the marinade also creates a subtly sweet and rich savory glaze.

½ cup (4 oz/125 g) white miso

¼ cup (2 fl oz/60 ml) mirin

¼ cup (2 fl oz/60 ml) sake

3 tablespoons sugar

1 teaspoon peeled and finely grated fresh ginger

6 sea bass fillets, about 6 oz (185 g) each, ¾–1 inch (2–2.5 cm) thick

1 teaspoon finely grated lemon zest

In a shallow glass baking dish, whisk together the miso, mirin, sake, sugar, and ginger until smooth to make a marinade. Add the sea bass and turn to coat evenly. Cover and refrigerate for at least 2 hours or up to overnight.

Preheat a broiler (grill).

Remove the sea bass from the marinade, reserving the marinade. Place the fillets on a broiler pan and broil (grill) 2–3 inches (5–7.5 cm) from the heat source until browned with crusty edges, about 4 minutes. Turn, brush with the reserved marinade, and broil until browned on the second side, 3–4 minutes.

Sprinkle with the lemon zest and serve.

Serves 6

Scallops and Papaya with Mango Sauce

For a more elaborate dish, add shrimp (prawns) to the skewers in addition to the scallops. When choosing a papaya, look for one that is spotted with yellow; a mango should have unblemished yellow skin blushed with pink.

In a food processor, combine the mango, olive oil, and lime juice. Process until smooth. Season with salt and pepper. The mixture should be tart; add more lime juice if it is too sweet.

In a nonaluminum bowl, combine $1/3$ cup (3 fl oz/80 ml) of the mango puree with the scallops. Toss to coat. Reserve the remaining puree for serving. Cover the scallops and refrigerate for 1 hour. Remove from the refrigerator 15 minutes before grilling.

At the same time soak 4 bamboo skewers in water to cover for 20–30 minutes.

Prepare a hot fire for a direct-heat cooking in a grill (see pages 8–9) Position the grill rack 4–6 inches (10–15 cm) above the fire.

Thread the scallops onto the skewers, alternating then with the papaya pieces and dividing them evenly among the skewers. Place the skewers on the rack. Cook, turning once, until the scallops are just opaque throughout when pierced with a knife, about 4 minutes on each side.

Transfer to a warmed serving platter or individual plates and brush the kabobs with the reserved mango puree. Serve hot.

Serves 4

1 large mango, peeled and pitted

1 tablespoon olive oil

Juice of 1 lime, or to taste

Salt and freshly ground pepper

24 sea scallops, about 1½ lb (750 g)

1 papaya, peeled, halved, seeded, and cut into pieces ½ inch (12 mm) thick

Grilled Shrimp and Sausage with Red Rice

1/2 cup (6 oz/185 g) apricot preserves

2 tablespoons olive oil

2 teaspoons lemon juice

2 teaspoons Dijon mustard

16 large shrimp (prawns), peeled and deveined

1 1/3 cups (10 oz/315 g) long-grain white rice

2 tablespoons unsalted butter

2 large red bell peppers (capsicums), roasted, peeled, seeded, and chopped

4 green (spring) onions, white parts and tender green tops chopped separately

2 teaspoons chili powder

1/2 teaspoon salt

1/4 cup (2 fl oz/60 ml) Chicken Stock (page 288) broth

1/2 cup (4 fl oz/125 ml) dry white wine

4 sweet Italian sausages, about 3/4 lb (375 g) total weight

1 tablespoon chopped fresh parsley

In a saucepan over medium heat, combine the preserves, oil, lemon juice, and mustard. Bring to a boil, pour into a nonaluminum bowl, and let cool. Add the shrimp, cover, and refrigerate for 3 hours. Remove from the refrigerator 30 minutes before grilling.

In a saucepan over medium-high heat, combine the rice and 2 2/3 cups (21 fl oz/660 ml) water. Bring to a boil, reduce the heat to low, cover, and cook until the rice is tender and the water is absorbed, about 18 minutes. Keep hot.

Meanwhile, in a saucepan over low heat, melt the butter. Add the white parts of the green onions and sauté until slightly softened, about 2 minutes. Stir in the chopped roasted peppers, chili powder, salt, and stock. Cover and cook until the peppers are soft, 3–4 minutes. Transfer to a food processor and blend until smooth. Return to the pan.

Prepare a hot fire for direct-heat cooking in a grill (sees page 8–9). Position the grill rack 4–6 inches (10–15 cm) above the fire. In a frying pan just big enough to hold the sausages in a single layer, bring the wine to a boil over high heat. Reduce the heat to medium, add the sausages, prick in several places with a fork, and cook, turning once, for 4 minutes total. Transfer the sausages to the grill rack. Cover the grill. Cook, turning once, until cooked through, about 5 minutes total.

Meanwhile, thread the shrimp onto metal skewers. Grill, turning once, until opaque throughout, 3–4 minutes on each side. Slice the sausages, add to the red pepper purée, and place over medium-low heat. Stir briefly, add the hot rice, and mix thoroughly. Toss in the shrimp and the reserved green onion tops. Transfer to a warmed serving bowl, sprinkle with the parsley, and serve.

Serves 4

Lobster with Basil Butter

Broiled, grilled, baked, or steamed, lobster's subtle sweetness and soft texture is perfectly enhanced by Charonnay. This simple, luxurious meal does not have to be reserved for a special occassion. Treat yourself on a warm summer night.

Bring a large pot three-fourths full of salted water to a rolling boil. Drop in the lobsters and, after the water returns to a boil, reduce the heat to medium-low. Simmer until almost cooked, 7–8 minutes. Using tongs, remove the lobsters. When cool enough to handle, and, working with 1 lobster at a time, insert the tip of a sharp knife into the point where the tail and body sections meet and cut through the tail. Continue to cut from the center through the head, cutting in half. Discard the green-black vein that runs the length of the body meat, as well as the small sand sac at the base of the head. If desired, reserve the green tomalley ("lobster butter") and any coral roe for using in the basil butter. Using a fork, pull out the tail meat in a single piece. Repeat with the other tail half. Set the meat aside. Twist off the claws from the body shell. Crack the claws and remove all the claw and knuckle meat. Cut the tail meat into 1-inch (2.5-cm) segments and return the meat, along with the claw and knuckle meat, to the tail shells. Preheat the oven to 350°F (180°C).

To make the basil butter, bring a saucepan three-fourths full of water to a boil. Add the basil leaves and blanch for 15 seconds. Drain, refresh in ice water, and drain again. Dry well with paper towels. In a blender or food processor, combine the basil, butter, and the tomalley and roe from the lobster, if using. Process until well incorporated. Season to taste with salt and pepper and with lemon juice, if using.

Spread the basil butter evenly on the lobster meat. Cover loosely with aluminum foil and roast until tender, 10–15 minutes. (The basil butter may darken). Remove from the oven, transfer to individual plates, and serve.

Serves 4

4 live lobsters, about 1½ lb (750 g) each

FOR THE BASIL BUTTER:

Leaves from 1 large bunch fresh basil, about 1½ cups (1½ oz/45 g leaves)

½ cup (4 oz/125 g) unsalted butter, at room temperature

Salt and freshly ground pepper

Lemon juice (optional)

Coconut Shrimp with Lime

If you lose some of the coconut coating as you skewer the shrimp, simply spoon on more before grilling. The shrimp also make great appetizers, in which case the recipe will serve 6. Serve with basmati rice and plenty of ice-cold beer.

3 limes

1/2 cup (2 oz/60 g) dried flaked coconut

1/2 cup (4 fl oz/125 ml) milk

1/4 cup (2 fl oz/60 ml) golden rum

1 tablespoon honey

24 extra-large shrimp (prawns), peeled and deveined

1 red onion, cut into 3/4-inch (2-cm) pieces

2 tablespoons olive oil

1/2 teaspoon chopped fresh tarragon

Cut 1 lime in half lengthwise, then cut crosswise into thin slices. Set aside. Grate enough zest from the remaining 2 limes to measure 1 teaspoon, then halve the zested limes and squeeze the juice from them.

In a food processor, combine the coconut, milk, rum, and honey. Process until the coconut is finely chopped but not puréed. Transfer to a large nonaluminum bowl and stir in the lime juice, lime zest, and shrimp. Mix well. Cover and refrigerate for 45 minutes. Remove from the refrigerator 15 minutes before grilling. At the same time, soak 6–8 bamboo skewers in water to cover for 20–30 minutes.

Meanwhile, in a bowl, combine the onion, olive oil, and tarragon. Mix well, cover, and set aside.

Prepare a medium-hot fire for direct-heat cooking in a grill (see pages 8–9). Position the grill rack 4–6 inches (10–15 cm) above the fire.

Remove the shrimp from the dish, taking care not to knock off any of the clinging marinade. Bend each shrimp almost in half and insert a skewer just above the tail so it passes through the body twice. Alternate the shrimp on the skewers with the lime slices and onion pieces.

Place the skewers on the grill rack. Cook, turning once, until the shrimp are crisp on the outside and opaque throughout, 4–5 minutes on each side.

Remove the shrimp, lime slices, and onion pieces from the skewers and place on a serving platter. Serve hot.

Serves 4

Vegetables & Sides

Summer Vegetables and Caponata with Polenta

FOR THE CAPONATA:

1 large eggplant (aubergine), about 1½lb (750 g), halved lengthwise

½ cup (4 fl oz/125 ml) olive oil

1 large white onion, chopped

1 tablespoon coarse salt

1½ teaspoons ground pepper

1 tablespoon extra-virgin olive oil

FOR THE POLENTA:

1 cup (5 oz/155 g) stone-ground yellow cornmeal

2 teaspoons salt

1 tablespoon unsalted butter

2 *each* zucchini (courgettes) and yellow summer squashes, cut lengthwise into eighths

1 large red onion, cut through the stem end into eighths

1 *each* green, yellow, and red, bell peppers (capsicums), seeded and cut lengthwise into eighths

About 2 tablespoons olive oil

2 tablespoons chopped fresh basil

¾ cup (1 oz/30 g) minced fresh flat-leaf (Italian) parsley

To make the caponata, preheat the oven to 450°F (230°C). Line a large baking pan with aluminum foil. Place the eggplant, cut sides down, on the prepared pan, and prick the skin with a fork in several places. Add a little water to the pan bottom. Roast the eggplant until soft to the touch, about 45 minutes. Scoop out the warm pulp; discard the skin. Roughly chop the pulp and transfer to a nonaluminum bowl.

In a large frying pan over medium heat, warm the olive oil. Add the onion and sauté until soft, about 8 minutes. Add the eggplant pulp and sauté, stirring occasionally, until the vegetables are tender, about 5 minutes. Season with the salt and pepper. Transfer to a nonaluminum container. Pour the extra-virgin olive oil on top to cover completely, cover, and chill for at least 2 hours.

To make the polenta; oil a rimmed baking sheet. In a saucepan over medium heat, bring 3 cups (24 fl oz/750 ml) water to a boil. In a bowl, whisk together 1 cup (8 fl oz/250 ml) water, the cornmeal, and the salt. Whisk the cornmeal mixture into the boiling water until it returns to a boil. Reduce the heat to low and cook, stirring every 10 minutes, until thick and creamy, about 40 minutes. If it becomes too thick, add a little more water. Stir in the butter and spread the cornmeal mixture evenly on the prepared sheet. Cover and chill for at least 1 hour to set.

Preheat the oven to 425°F (220°C). Keeping the vegetables separate, place them in a single layer on two baking sheets lined with parchment paper. Drizzle with olive oil, and sprinkle with the basil. Roast until tender, 20–30 minutes. Keep warm.

Cut the polenta into 24 diamonds. Spray a stove-top grill pan with nonstick cooking spray and warm over high heat. Add the polenta and grill, turning once, until crisp, about 8 minutes total. Spoon caponata into the center of each plate. Add polenta triangles and roasted vegetables. Sprinkle parsley over the top. Serve warm.

Serves 8

Grilled Asparagus with Parmesan Cheese

Fat spears of asparagus are the best choice for grilling. They're easier to handle and less likely to fall through the grill rack. Savory Parmesan and fresh herbs make delicious partners for the tender, caramelized asparagus spears.

Snap the tough stem ends off the asparagus spears. Using a vegetable peeler and starting about 2 inches (5 cm) below the tip, peel off the thick outer skin. Place the stalks in a shallow nonaluminum dish.

In a small bowl, stir together the olive oil, green onion, tarragon, and parsley. Pour over the asparagus. Toss to coat. Cover and let stand at room temperature for 30 minutes.

Prepare a medium-hot fire for direct-heat cooking in a grill (see pages 8–9). Position the grill rack 4–6 inches (10–15 cm) above the fire.

Place the asparagus on the rack. Cook, turning once, until lightly browned, about 8 minutes total. Then continue to cook, turning several times (use the outer edges of the grill rack if the spears begin to burn), until tender-crisp, about 10 minutes longer. Transfer to a serving dish and sprinkle with the Parmesan cheese. Serve immediately.

Serves 4

1½ lb (750 g) thick asparagus

¼ cup (2 fl oz/60 ml) olive oil

1 green (spring) onion, minced

1 tablespoon fresh tarragon leaves

2 teaspoons chopped fresh parsley

¼ cup (1 oz/30 g) grated Parmesan cheese

Baked Tomatoes and Zucchini

Sautéed red onions form an aromatic base for this Mediterranean-inspired side dish. Look for plum tomatoes and zucchini with similar diameters so that you have uniform slices to arrange attractively atop the onions.

2 tablespoons pure olive oil

1 red onion, sliced

Salt and freshly ground pepper

3/4 lb (375 g) plum (Roma) tomatoes, sliced

2 small zucchini (courgettes), about 3/4 lb (375 g) total weight, sliced

1 tablespoon minced fresh basil

1 tablespoon minced fresh marjoram

1/4 cup (2 fl oz/60 ml) water or Chicken Stock (page 288)

Preheat the oven to 350°F (180°C). Butter or oil a shallow 2-qt (2-l) baking dish.

In a frying pan over medium heat, warm the oil. Add the onion and sauté slowly until very soft and beginning to brown, about 10 minutes. Transfer the sautéed onion slices to the prepared baking dish, spreading them evenly over the bottom. Season with salt and pepper.

Arrange the tomato slices and zucchini slices over the onion in alternating rows. Sprinkle with the basil and marjoram and season with salt and pepper. Pour the stock or water evenly over the vegetables.

Cover and bake until the vegetables are bubbling and tender, about 40 minutes. Remove from the oven, uncover, and serve hot directly from the dish.

Serves 4–6

Rustic Grilled Potatoes

Potatoes are superb prepared on a grill. Here, the potatoes are parboiled and marinated in a vinaigrette dressing before grilling. You'll need a large, rectangular hinged grill basket for this recipe.

In a small bowl, mash the garlic and salt with the back of a spoon to form a paste. Stir in the mustard. Slowly whisk in the olive oil, lemon juice, vinegar, paprika, and rosemary to make a vinaigrette. Set aside.

Bring a saucepan three-fourths full of salted water to a boil. Add the red and white potatoes and parboil for 5 minutes. Drain. While the potatoes are still slightly warm, cut them in half. Place in a large bowl and drizzle with the vinaigrette. Using a sturdy rubber spatula, toss gently, coating the potatoes evenly with the vinaigrette. Cover and let stand at room temperature for 30 minutes.

Prepare a medium-hot fire for direct-heat cooking in a grill (see pages 8–9). Position the grill rack 4–6 inches (10–15 cm) above the fire.

Place the potatoes about 2 deep in a lightly oiled rectangular hinged grill basket. Place the basket on the grill rack and cook the potatoes, turning once, until tender and nicely browned, about 10 minutes on each side.

Transfer the potatoes to a warmed serving dish and serve hot.

Serves 4

1 clove garlic, minced

1/2 teaspoon coarse salt

1 teaspoon Dijon mustard

1/3 cup (3 fl oz/80 ml) olive oil

1 tablespoon lemon juice

2 teaspoons red wine vinegar

1 teaspoon Hungarian sweet paprika

1/2 teaspoon chopped fresh rosemary

3/4 lb (375 g) small red potatoes

3/4 lb (375 g) small white potatoes

Grilled Stuffed Portobello Mushrooms on Porcini Couscous

Portobello mushrooms are available year-round, so you can make this elegant vegetarian main course in any season. Serve with a light red wine, such as Pinot Noir, which has an earthy quality that pairs well with savory mushrooms.

4 fresh portobello mushrooms, each 3–4 inches (7.5–10 cm) in diameter

3 tablespoons extra-virgin olive oil

1 shallot, minced

½ cup (4 fl oz/125 ml) Vegetable Stock (page 288) or broth

1 sweet potato, peeled and coarsely grated

½ lb (250 g) spinach leaves, coarsely chopped

Salt and freshly ground pepper

½ cup (¼ lb/125 g) part-skim ricotta cheese

¼ cup (4 oz/125 g) dried porcini, soaked in 2 cups (16 fl oz/500 ml) warm Vegetable Stock (page 288) for 20 minutes

1 cup (5 oz/155 g) couscous

2 tablespoons minced fresh flat-leaf (Italian) parsley

1 teaspoon minced fresh thyme

Prepare a medium-hot fire for direct-heat cooking in a grill (see pages 8–9). Position the grill rack about 4 inches (10 cm) above the fire. Lightly oil the grill rack.

Brush the portobello mushrooms clean, then cut off the stems and remove the dark gills. Set the mushroom caps aside.

In a sauté pan over medium heat, warm the olive oil. Add the shallot and sauté until softened, about 3 minutes. Add the stock, raise the heat to high, and bring to a boil. Reduce the heat to medium and add the sweet potato. Cook uncovered, stirring occasionally, until tender, 5–8 minutes. Add the spinach and cook until wilted, 4–5 minutes. Season with salt and pepper. Remove from the heat.

Add the ricotta to the spinach mixture and stir to combine. Spoon the mixture into the mushroom caps, dividing it evenly. Place the mushrooms, filled sides up, on the grill rack and grill until completely heated through, about 10 minutes.

Meanwhile, drain the porcini, reserving the soaking liquid. Chop the porcini and set aside. Strain the liquid through a fine-mesh sieve lined with a double thickness of cheesecloth (muslin) into a saucepan. Bring to a boil, add the couscous, parsley, and thyme, and remove from the heat. Cover and let stand for 5 minutes. Uncover and add the chopped porcini. Fluff with a fork and season with salt and pepper. Keep warm until the grilled mushrooms are ready.

Spoon the couscous onto a warmed serving platter and arrange the stuffed mushrooms on top. Serve immediately.

Serves 4

Oven-Baked Brown Rice with Roast Tomatoes

8 firm yet ripe plum (Roma) tomatoes, seeded and coarsely chopped

Coarse salt

1 teaspoon unsalted butter

2 tablespoons olive oil

1 yellow onion, chopped

2 cups (14 oz/440 g) short-grain brown rice

1 tablespoon chopped fresh thyme, plus sprigs for garnish

Freshly ground pepper

4¼ cups (34 fl oz/1 l) Chicken Stock (page 288) or broth, heated

Preheat the oven to 400°F (200°C). Line a rimmed baking sheet with aluminum foil. Sprinkle the tomatoes with salt to taste and spread them out on the prepared baking sheet. Roast until the edges of the skins are browned but not burned, 10–12 minutes. Remove from the oven and set aside. Reduce the oven temperature to 375°F (190°C).

Meanwhile, in a Dutch oven or a large, heavy ovenproof saucepan with a lid over medium heat, melt the butter with the oil. Add the onion and sauté until soft and translucent, about 5 minutes. Add the rice and chopped thyme and season with salt and pepper to taste. Continue to cook, stirring constantly, until the rice is shiny, about 3 minutes.

Stir in the roasted tomatoes, then pour in the hot stock. Stir once, cover, and bring to a boil. Transfer to the oven and cook, covered, until all the liquid is absorbed, 40–45 minutes. To test for doneness, tilt the baking dish to one side. If the rice moves, continue cooking until all the liquid is absorbed; if the rice clings to the top edges of the baking dish, it is done.

Remove the rice from the oven and fluff with a fork. Transfer to a warmed serving bowl. Garnish with thyme sprigs and serve immediately.

Serves 8

Green Tomato and Fresh Corn Pie

Preheat the oven to 425°F (220°C). Butter a shallow 1 1/2 -qt (1.5-l) baking dish.

Seed and mince the pepper and chile. Pit and coarsely chop the olives. Remove the sausages from the casings. In a frying pan over medium heat, cook the sausages, using a wooden spoon to stir often and break up the meat, until cooked through and somewhat crumbly, about 5 minutes. Transfer to paper towels to drain. Pour off any excess fat in the pan, leaving a scant 1/4 teaspoon. Return the pan to medium heat and add the onion, bell pepper, and chile. Cook, stirring often, until the vegetables begin to soften, 3–4 minutes. Transfer to a bowl, and add the sausage, corn kernels, and olives; stir to mix. Set aside.

In a bowl, stir together the flour, cornmeal, salt, and pepper. Add the green tomatoes and turn to coat with the flour mixture. In a sauté pan over medium-high heat, melt the butter with the oil. When the butter foams, use a slotted spoon to transfer the tomatoes to the sauté pan. Do not add the accumulated juices in the bottom of the bowl. Cook, stirring, until the tomatoes have browned slightly, 3–4 minutes. Turn and cook until golden brown, 2–3 minutes longer. Transfer to a plate and set aside.

To make the topping, in a bowl, stir together the cornmeal, flour, thyme, baking powder, salt, and pepper. Stir in the eggs, milk, and oil and mix just until thoroughly moistened.

Pour the sausage mixture into the prepared dish, spreading evenly. Top with the green tomatoes, again spreading evenly. Pour the topping evenly over the tomatoes.

Bake until the topping is slightly puffed and cooked throughout, 15–20 minutes. Remove from the oven, cover loosely with aluminum foil, and let stand for 10–15 minutes. Scoop from the dish to serve.

Serves 4–6

1 *each* red bell pepper (capsicum) and jalapeno chile

12 tart green or black olives

1/3 lb (155 g) chicken sausages

1/2 yellow onion, minced

Kernels from 2 ears of corn

1/4 cup (1 1/2 oz/45 g) all-purpose (plain) flour

2 tablespoons fine cornmeal

1/2 teaspoon *each* salt and freshly ground pepper

5 large green tomatoes, diced

1 1/2 tablespoons unsalted butter

2 tablespoons vegetable oil

FOR THE TOPPING:

3/4 cup (4 oz/125 g) fine cornmeal

2 tablespoons all-purpose (plain) flour

2 tablespoons fresh thyme leaves

1 teaspoon baking powder

1/2 teaspoon each salt and ground pepper

2 eggs, beaten

1/2 cup (4 fl oz/125 ml) milk

1 tablespoon vegetable oil

Butter-Roasted Corn on the Cob

Corn on the cob is classic all-American summer fare, but roasting it with butter and marjoram brings out a nutty flavor and adds a dash of sophistication. Double or triple this recipe to serve a crowd, and roast some vegetables to accompany the corn.

Adjust an oven rack to the center position in the oven without another rack above it. Preheat the oven to 325°F (165°C).

Pull off the husk from around each ear of corn. With a dry vegetable brush, brush away the silk from between the kernel rows. Rinse the husked corn under cold running water, drain, and dry well with paper towels.

Put the butter, marjoram, salt, and pepper in a small bowl. Beat with a fork until well combined. Put 4 sheets of aluminum foil on a work surface and set 1 ear of corn on each piece of foil. Spread the seasoned butter over each ear of corn, dividing the butter equally among the 4 ears. Wrap each ear of corn completely in its piece of foil. Be careful not to leave any open spaces.

Place the wrapped corn on the rack in the oven. Roast the corn for 15 minutes. With the metal tongs, turn over each ear of corn. Roast the corn 15 minutes longer, until lightly charred in places.

Place corn on a serving platter, carefully unwrapping the hot foil. Serve immediately.

Serves 4

4 ears of corn

3 tablespoons unsalted butter, softened

1/2 teaspoon dried marjoram

1/4 teaspoon salt

1/8 teaspoon freshly ground pepper

Sweet Potato Oven Fries

No matter how many of these crisp, sweet, and aromatic fries you cook, don't count on leftovers. You can bake the sweet potatoes at any temperature required for a roast; the cooking time will be longer at lower temperatures.

About 1/2 cup (4 fl oz/125 ml) vegetable oil

6–8 large orange-fleshed sweet potatoes

About 2 teaspoons ground cumin, or to taste

Coarse salt and freshly ground pepper

Preheat the oven to 425°F (220°C).

Line 2 or 3 rimmed baking sheets with aluminum foil. Generously spread the vegetable oil on the pan bottoms, dividing it evenly.

Peel the sweet potatoes. Using a sharp knife, cut the sweet potatoes lengthwise into narrow strips about $1/4$ inch (6 mm) thick. As the sticks are cut, immediately roll them in the oil on the baking sheets to prevent them from turning black. When all the sticks have been coated, spread them out on the sheets in a single layer.

Sprinkle the sweet potatoes in each pan with about $1/2$ teaspoon of the cumin and salt to taste.

Roast until crisp on the outside and tender on the inside, 25–30 minutes. Transfer to 2 or 3 layers of paper towels to drain briefly. Sprinkle with salt, pepper, and 1–$1$$1/2$ teaspoons cumin, or to taste. Transfer to a warmed dish and serve immediately.

Serves 6–8

Baby Artichokes with Sunflower Seeds

Use only the freshest and smallest artichokes for this tasty dish. Serve as a starter, side dish, or as part of a salad platter. You can roast the artichokes at any temperature required for another dish, adjusting the cooking time as necessary.

Preheat the oven to 425°F (220°C). Oil the bottom of a baking dish or large enough to hold the artichokes in a single layer with the 2 tablespoons olive oil.

Fill a large bowl with water and add the juice of 1 lemon. Cut the remaining 2 lemons in half. Working with 1 artichoke at a time, cut off the stem even with the base. Break off the tough outer leaves until you reach the paler inner green leaves. Cut off the prickly tops of the leaves, then cut the artichokes in half lengthwise. Immediately rub the exposed parts with the cut side of a lemon half. Drop the artichokes into the lemon water. Repeat until all the artichokes are trimmed.

Add the sunflower seeds to a small, dry frying pan over high heat and shake the pan until seeds are fragrant, about 3 minutes. Transfer to a food processor. Pulse to chop coarsely, then transfer to a small bowl. Add the 1 teaspoon chives, summer savory, and salt and pepper to taste. Mix well; set aside.

Drain the artichokes and pat dry. Roll the artichokes in the oil in the prepared dish, coating each artichoke half completely. Arrange the artichokes, cut sides down, in the pan and roast until the leaves are lightly browned and the hearts are still firm, 10–12 minutes. Turn over the artichokes, sprinkle the sunflower-seed mixture evenly over the top, and then spoon some oil from the dish over the seed mixture. Continue to roast, basting with oil from the dish once or twice, until the edges are browned and crisp and the hearts are fork tender, about 20 minutes longer. Sprinkle with salt.

Transfer to a warmed platter, garnish with chives, and serve immediately.

Serves 6

2 tablespoons extra-virgin olive oil

3 lemons

8 baby artichokes, each 1½–2¼ inches (4–5.5 cm) in diameter

2 tablespoons shelled sunflower seeds

1 teaspoon snipped fresh chives, plus extra for garnish

½ teaspoon dried summer savory

Coarse salt and freshly ground pepper

Mushroom and Spinach Salad

Hinged grill baskets make it possible to grill just about anything—even spinach. This unusual salad is best served the moment the ingredients come off the grill. Cremini, porcini, or shiitakes can be used in place of the portobellos.

1 lb (500 g) fresh small portobello mushrooms, brushed clean and stems removed

1/4 cup (2 fl oz/60 ml) safflower oil

1 teaspoon chopped fresh sage

1/2 teaspoon freshly ground pepper

1/4 cup (1 oz/30 g) walnuts

10 oz (315 g) spinach, stems removed

2 tablespoons walnut oil

3 teaspoons lemon juice

2 teaspoons red wine vinegar

In a bowl, lightly toss the mushrooms with the safflower oil, sage, and pepper. Cover and let stand at room temperature for 20 minutes.

Meanwhile, preheat the oven to 350°F (180°C). Spread the walnuts on a baking sheet and toast until they are lightly browned and fragrant, 5–7 minutes. Remove from the oven, chop coarsely, and set aside.

Prepare a hot fire for direct-heat cooking in a grill (see pages 8–9). Position the grill rack 4–6 inches (10–15 cm) above the fire. Oil the grill rack.

Place the mushrooms on the rack, gill side down. (If the mushrooms are quite small, put them in a lightly oiled hinged grill basket.) Cook until lightly browned, about 3 minutes. Turn and continue to cook until browned and just tender, about 4 minutes longer. Transfer to a plate.

Arrange the spinach leaves over the bottom of a lightly oiled hinged grill basket. Close the basket and sprinkle each side with 1 tablespoon of the walnut oil, 1 1/2 teaspoons of the lemon juice, and 1 teaspoon of the vinegar.

Place the basket on the rack. Cook the spinach, turning once, just until slightly wilted, about 3 minutes on each side. Transfer to a serving bowl.

Slice the mushrooms about 1/8 inch (3 mm) thick. Add to the spinach leaves along with the toasted walnuts. Toss to mix. Serve immediately.

Serves 4

Balsamic Vidalia Blossoms

Roasting slowly caramelizes the natural sugars in onions, giving them a rich, sweet flavor that is highlighted by the balsamic vinegar. The onions are a nice complement to roasted meats and fowl, and make a splendid addition to an antipasto platter.

Preheat the oven to 400°F (200°C). Oil the bottom of a baking dish or pie dish large enough to hold the onions in a single layer.

Working with 1 onion at a time, peel the skin from the top of the onion, trimming off the long hairs but leaving the root end intact. Using a sharp knife and starting at the stem end, cut the onion into eighths or tenths almost through to the root end. Be careful not to cut all the way through. Using your thumbs, pull the onion open slightly to form a blossom shape. Set the onions, root ends down, in the prepared dish; they should be touching but not packed too tightly. Season with salt and pepper to taste, then drizzle with the vinegar and olive oil.

Roast until onions are tender when pierced with a fork and the tips are browned, about 35 minutes. Transfer to a warmed platter and garnish with the parsley. Serve immediately.

Serves 8

8 large Vidalia or other sweet onions

Coarse salt and freshly ground pepper

2 tablespoons balsamic vinegar

About 1½ tablespoons olive oil

⅓ cup (½ oz/15 g) chopped fresh flat-leaf (Italian) parsley

Sautéed Apples with Bacon and Caramelized Onions

This simple combination of apples, onions, and bacon is an excellent quick dish to serve as a side dish with grilled or roasted meats. The tart apples are balanced by the sweet onions and smoky bacon. Serve on its own or with buttered black bread.

1 teaspoon unsalted butter

1 tablespoon olive oil

1¹/₂ lb (750 g) Canadian bacon, thinly sliced

4 large yellow onions, sliced

4 large tart, red apples such as Macoun or Jonathan, cored and cut crosswise into rings ¹/₂ inch (12 mm) thick, plus 1 apple, cored and thinly sliced lengthwise

Freshly ground pepper

In a large, heavy sauté pan over medium-high heat, melt the butter with the oil. When the foam subsides, add the bacon and sauté until lightly browned and crisp, 5–10 minutes. Using a slotted spoon, transfer to paper towels to drain; set aside.

In the same pan over medium heat, sauté the onions in the fat remaining in the pan until soft, about 8 minutes. Add the apple rings and cover the pan. Reduce the heat to low and cook, shaking the pan gently, until the apples are nearly soft but still keep their shape, about 6 minutes. Return the bacon to the pan, cover, and cook until the bacon is hot, about 4 minutes. Season generously with pepper.

Transfer the bacon, onions, and apples to a warmed platter and garnish with the thin apple slices. Serve immediately.

Serves 8

Niçoise Mushrooms

Roast mushrooms are the perfect accompaniment to prepare while roasting meat. As a serving alternative, chop the roasted mushrooms together with enough of the cooking liquid to bind them, season to taste, and serve the resulting pâté on toast points.

Preheat the oven to 400°F (200°C). Spread the olive oil on the bottom of a baking dish large enough to hold the mushrooms in a single layer.

Place the anchovies in a single layer in a small shallow bowl. Add enough milk to nearly cover them and let stand for 5–10 minutes. Drain off the milk and discard. Pat the anchovies dry with paper towels, removing any tiny bones in the process.

On a cutting board, chop together the anchovies, garlic, rosemary, thyme, and lavender until the mixture is evenly minced but not reduced to a paste.

Place the mushrooms in the prepared baking dish and toss to coat evenly with the oil. Sprinkle the anchovy mixture evenly over the mushrooms. Season with salt and pepper to taste.

Roast the mushrooms until tender, 15–17 minutes depending upon their size. Remove from the oven and transfer to a warmed serving dish. Serve hot.

Serves 6–8

2 tablespoons olive oil

4 salt-cured anchovies, halved and filleted

About 2 tablespoons milk

2 large cloves garlic, chopped

1/2 teaspoon dried rosemary

1/2 teaspoon dried thyme

1/2 teaspoon dried lavender

1 1/2 lb (750 g) fresh button mushrooms, brushed clean and stems removed

Coarse salt and freshly ground pepper

Catalan Mixed Grilled Vegetables

This tapa, known as *escalivada*, comes from the region of Catalonia in northeastern Spain. Make it in late summer, when the vegetables are at their peak. Serve with crusty bread and an assortment of Spanish cheeses, such as Manchego, and serrano ham.

4 Asian (slender) eggplants (aubergines), 1–1¼ lb (500–625 g) total weight

5 small, ripe tomatoes

1 red bell pepper (capsicum)

1 green bell pepper (capsicum)

1 yellow onion, halved

5 tablespoons (2½ fl oz/75 ml) extra-virgin olive oil

Salt and freshly ground pepper

3 tablespoons chopped fresh flat-leaf (Italian) parsley

2 cloves garlic, coarsely chopped

Prepare a medium-hot fire for direct-heat cooking in a charcoal grill (see pages 8–9). Position the grill rack 4–5 inches (10–13 cm) above the fire. At the same time, preheat the oven to 350°F (180 °C).

Place the eggplants, tomatoes, bell peppers, and onion on the grill rack. Grill, turning occasionally, until blackened, 8–10 minutes.

Remove all the vegetables from the grill. Cut the tomatoes in half crosswise and place them, cut sides up, in a baking pan. Add the eggplants, peppers, and onion to the pan and drizzle all the vegetables with 1 tablespoon of the oil.

Roast until the tomatoes collapse, about 20 minutes. Remove the pan from the oven, transfer the tomatoes to a bowl, and cover the bowl with plastic wrap. Return the remaining vegetables to the oven and roast until the eggplants and peppers collapse and are completely tender, about 30 minutes longer. Again remove the pan from the oven and transfer the peppers and eggplants to the bowl holding the tomatoes. Return the onion to the oven and continue to roast until soft, 15–20 minutes longer. Remove from the oven and transfer the onion to the bowl holding the peppers, eggplants, and tomatoes. Let stand for 15 minutes.

Peel away the skins from the peppers, then discard the stems and seeds. Slice the peppers into long, narrow strips. Peel the eggplants and tear into thin strips. Pour the remaining 4 tablespoons (2 fl oz/60 ml) olive oil evenly over the top. Combine the parsley and garlic and sprinkle over the vegetables. Serve warm.

Serves 6

Stuffed Crookneck Squash

Filled with a curry-flavored mixture of chopped squash, chicken, and prosciutto, these stuffed squashes make a fine light meal accompanied by crusty bread and a green salad.

4 yellow crookneck squashes, about 1/2 lb (250 g) each

2 tablespoons unsalted butter

2 green (spring) onions, white parts and tender green tops chopped separately

1 small clove garlic, minced

3/4 cup (41/2 oz/140 g) diced cooked chicken

1/3 cup (2 oz/60 g) chopped prosciutto

1 tablespoon curry powder

1/2 teaspoon salt

1/4 teaspoon freshly ground pepper

1/4 cup (1 oz/30 g) pine nuts, toasted

Using a sharp knife, cut a thin slice off the entire length of each squash. Finely chop the slice and transfer it to a bowl.

Cut several slashes across the exposed flesh of each squash. Then, with a teaspoon, gently scoop out the flesh from the squashes, leaving shells about $^1/_{16}$ inch (2 mm) thick. Do not puncture the skins. Finely chop the flesh and add to the bowl.

Bring a saucepan three-fourths full of salted water to a boil, add the squash shells, and parboil for 30 seconds. Using tongs, carefully remove and invert to drain.

In a frying pan over medium-low heat, melt the butter. Add the white parts of the green onions and sauté until beginning to soften, about 1 minute. Add the garlic and sauté until translucent, about 2 minutes longer. Stir in the chopped squash and continue to cook, stirring frequently, until softened, about 5 minutes. Add the chicken, prosciutto, curry powder, salt, pepper, and pine nuts. Mix well and remove from the heat. Spoon the mixture into the squash shells, dividing it evenly. Sprinkle evenly with the green onion tops.

Prepare a hot fire for direct-heat cooking in a covered grill (see pages 8–9). Position the grill rack 4–6 inches (10–15 cm) above the fire. Place the squashes on the rack. Cover the grill and open the vents halfway. Cook until the squashes are lightly browned and tender when pierced with a knife, about 20 minutes. Transfer to individual plates and serve hot.

Serves 4

Garden-Style Eggplant Parmesan

Although this dish can be made throughout the summer, it is an especially good season ender. Late-harvest tomatoes ripened to a dark red make a sauce that is sublimely sweet and full of flavor.

To make the sauce, in a large saucepan over medium heat, warm the olive oil. Add the garlic and sauté until translucent, 2–3 minutes. Add the tomatoes and oregano, raise the heat to high, and bring to a boil. Reduce the heat to medium-low and simmer, uncovered, until the tomatoes have cooked down, 30–40 minutes. Season to taste with salt.

Preheat the oven to 450°F (230°C).

Place the eggplant slices in a single layer on a large baking sheet. Drizzle evenly on both sides with the olive oil. Top with the thyme and place in the oven. Cook until lightly browned, about 10 minutes. Turn and cook until lightly browned on the second side, 5–6 minutes longer. Place under a preheated broiler (grill) until a slightly golden crust forms on the tops of the slices, 2–3 minutes. Turn and broil (grill) on the second side until golden, 2–3 minutes longer.

Reduce the oven temperature to 400°F (200°C). Arrange one-third of the eggplant slices in a shallow 2-qt (2-l) baking dish. Top with one-third each of the sauce, mozzarella, oregano, and Parmesan. Repeat the layers twice, beginning with the eggplant. Dot the top with the butter.

Bake for 15 minutes. Remove the dish from the oven and carefully tip it, pressing on the surface with a spoon or spatula. Pour off any excess juice. Return to the oven and bake until the top is lightly browned and bubbling, 15–20 minutes longer. Remove from the oven, cover loosely with aluminum foil, and let stand for 10 minutes. Scoop from the dish to serve.

Serves 4–6

FOR THE SAUCE:

2 tablespoons olive oil

2 cloves garlic, chopped

3 lb (1.5 kg) fully ripe tomatoes, peeled and coarsely chopped

1 tablespoon chopped fresh oregano

Salt

4 or 5 small or 2 medium eggplants (aubergines), cut into slices 1/2 inch (12 mm) thick

4 tablespoons (2 fl oz/60 ml) extra-virgin olive oil

2 tablespoons fresh thyme leaves

6 oz (185 g) mozzarella cheese, shredded

1/4 cup (1/3 oz/10 g) chopped fresh oregano

1/4 cup (1 oz/30 g) grated Parmesan cheese

1 1/2 tablespoons unsalted butter, cut into bits

Sautéed Potatoes

This timeless dish is updated using a variety of potatoes for an interesting mix of color and texture. It is a delicious accompaniment to any roasted meat dish, and would be equally welcome at a casual buffet or a sit-down feasts with friends and family.

6 small Yukon gold potatoes

6 fingerling potatoes

6 small red potatoes

10 green (spring) onions, including the tender green topscut into ¹/₂-inch (12-mm) lengths

1 tablespoon chopped fresh winter savory or 1 teaspoon dried winter savory

5 tablespoons (2¹/₂ oz/75 g) unsalted butter

¹/₄ cup (2 fl oz/60 ml) vegetable oil

Salt and freshly ground pepper

¹/₄ cup (¹/₃ oz/10 g) chopped flat-leaf (Italian) parsley for garnish

Have ready a large bowl of cold water. Peel the Yukon gold potatoes, cut them into slices ¹/8 inch (3 mm) thick, and immediately drop the slices into the water. Cut, but do not peel the remaining potatoes the same thickness and add the slices to the water. (The potatoes can be left in the water for up to 4 hours before cooking.) Drain and pat dry with paper towels just before sautéing.

In a bowl, toss the green onions with the savory. In a large, heavy cast-iron frying pan over high heat, melt the butter with the vegetable oil. When the foam subsides, add the potatoes in batches alternately with the green onions, season with salt and pepper, and allow an even brown crust to form on the bottom, 8–10 minutes. Using a metal spatula, turn the potatoes over, shaking the pan to redistribute the potatoes. If necessary, add more oil and adjust the heat to prevent burning. Continue cooking until browned on the bottom, about 5 minutes.

Reduce the heat to medium-low, cover, and cook until the potatoes are almost tender, about 10 minutes. Uncover, raise the heat to medium-high, and carefully turn often until the potatoes are cooked through, about 5 minutes longer.

Season the potatoes with salt and pepper, sprinkle with parsley, and serve hot.

Serves 6

Cheese-Herb Hominy Grits

Robust in flavor and texture yet low in fat, these grits make a great accompaniment to hearty main courses. You can use this same recipe to make a soft-style polenta; cook the polenta until it pulls away from the sides of the pot, about 20 minutes.

In a saucepan over medium heat, warm the corn oil. Add the onion and sauté until soft, about 5 minutes. Stir in the grits and then whisk in the stock. Season to taste with salt and pepper. Simmer uncovered, whisking occasionally, until the grits are thick and translucent, about 10 minutes.

Whisk in the buttermilk and cook until incorporated, about 2 minutes longer. Add the cheese, chives, and basil, and continue whisking until incorporated. Taste and adjust the seasonings.

Transfer the grits to a warmed serving dish and serve immediately.

Serves 4

2 teaspoons corn oil

1/2 small yellow onion, chopped

3/4 cup (4 1/2 oz/140 g) quick-cooking hominy grits

2 cups (16 fl oz/500 ml) Chicken Stock (page 288)

Salt and freshly ground pepper

1/4 cup (2 fl oz/60 ml) low-fat buttermilk

2 tablespoons fresh goat cheese

2 tablespoons snipped fresh chives

2 tablespoons chopped fresh basil

Buttermilk Chive Biscuits

High rising and incredibly rich, these biscuits are at their best when eaten straight out of the oven. Quick to make, they're the perfect last-minute accompaniment to any meal, especially Southern-Style dishes like Classic Barbecued Chicken (page 101).

2 cups (10 oz/315 g) all-purpose (plain) flour

2 tablespoons sugar

1¹/₂ tablespoons baking powder

¹/₂ teaspoon salt

¹/₂ cup (4 oz/125 g) chilled unsalted butter, cut into thin slivers

1 whole egg, plus 1 egg yolk

Scant 1 cup (8 fl oz/250 ml) buttermilk, or as needed

¹/₄ cup (¹/₃ oz/10 g) snipped fresh chives

Preheat the oven to 400°F (200°C).

In a bowl, stir together the flour, sugar, baking powder, and salt. Add the butter and, using a pastry blender or 2 knives, cut the butter into the flour mixture until the mixture resembles coarse meal.

In a measuring pitcher, combine the egg and egg yolk and whisk until blended. Add enough buttermilk to measure 1 cup (8 fl oz/250 ml). Whisk in the snipped chives. Add the buttermilk mixture to the flour mixture. Using a fork, mix quickly just until the dry ingredients are absorbed.

Turn out the dough onto a heavily floured work surface and knead gently and quickly until the dough is no longer sticky, about 5 minutes. Pat the dough into a square or rectangle ¹/₂ inch (12 mm) thick. Dip a round biscuit cutter 3 inches (7.5 cm) in diameter in flour and cut out 24 rounds from the dough. Arrange the rounds on ungreased baking sheets about 1 inch (2.5 cm) apart. Bake until golden brown, 12–15 minutes. Remove from the oven and serve hot or warm.

Makes 24 biscuits

Roasted Carrots, Parsnips, and Garlic with Thyme

Add a splash of color to any holiday meal with carrots and parsnips, a perfect partnership
of flavor and texture. In this oven-roasted dish, the root vegetables cook along with
whole garlic cloves until caramelized and soft. Thyme makes an ideal herbal accent.

Preheat the oven to 350°F (180°C).

In a 10-inch (25-cm) pie dish or baking dish, combine the parsnips, carrots, and
garlic. If using fresh thyme, add half at this time. If using dried thyme, add it all,
then season with salt and pepper. Toss to blend. Dot with the butter.

Roast the vegetables, stirring occasionally, until the vegetables are tender and
lightly browned, about 55 minutes. Season with salt and pepper to taste and add
the remaining fresh thyme leaves, if using. Transfer to a serving dish and garnish
with thyme sprigs, if using. Serve warm.

Serves 6–8

1 lb (500 g) parsnips, peeled
and cut on the diagonal into
slices 1/2-inch (12 mm) thick

1 lb (500 g) carrots, peeled and
cut on the diagonal into slices
1/2-inch (12-mm) thick

12 cloves garlic, peeled but left
whole

1 tablespoon fresh thyme
leaves or 1 teaspoon dried
thyme, plus fresh sprigs for
garnish (optional)

Salt and freshly ground pepper

1/4 cup (2 oz/60 g) unsalted
butter, cut into small pieces

Mediterranean Salad Platter

Mediterranean vegetables, cheese, olives, and anchovies come together in this easy outdoor dish. To serve the salad, simply arrange the elements on a platter and drizzle with the dressing.

4 medium zucchini (courgettes), thinly sliced lengthwise

3 red bell peppers (capsicums)

2 tablespoons olive oil

4 large tomatoes, sliced

2 large red onions, thinly sliced

6 oz (185 g) feta cheese, crumbled

1/2 cup (2 1/2 oz/75 g) each Mediterranean-style oil-packed black olives, Kalamata olives, and Mediterranean-style green olives

2 tablespoons capers

6 anchovy fillets packed in olive oil, drained (optional)

FOR THE DRESSING:

1/2 cup (4 fl oz/125 ml) extra-virgin olive oil

1/3 cup (3 fl oz/80 ml) balsamic vinegar

1/2 teaspoon salt

1/2 teaspoon freshly ground pepper

Prepare a hot fire for direct-heat cooking in a grill (see pages 8–9). Position the grill rack 4–6 inches (10–15 cm) above the fire. Brush the zucchini and bell peppers with the olive oil.

Place the zucchini directly on the grill rack or in a grill basket on the rack and grill until lightly golden on the first side, 4–5 minutes. Turn and cook until golden on the second side, about 3 minutes longer. At the same time, place the bell peppers directly on the grill rack and grill, turning as necessary, until the skins are evenly blackened and blistered, 4–5 minutes on each side. Remove the zucchini and set aside. Place the peppers on a plate, cover with aluminum foil, let stand for 10 minutes, and then peel away the skins. Cut the peppers in half lengthwise and remove the seeds. Cut the halves lengthwise into thin strips.

To serve, arrange the grilled zucchini, bell peppers, tomato slices, and onion slices on a platter. Top with the feta cheese, all the olives, the capers, and anchovies, if using.

To make the dressing, in a bowl, combine the olive oil, balsamic vinegar, salt, and pepper; mix well. Drizzle the dressing evenly over the salad and serve.

Serves 6–8

Corn Salad

This salad is a popular one for late-summer barbecues, when corn and tomatoes are at their seasonal best. To turn this salad into a light main course, add diced cooked chicken and serve on lettuce leaves.

Bring a large saucepan three-fourths full of water to a boil. Add the corn and boil until just slightly cooked, about 3 minutes. Drain, rinse under cold running water, and pat dry. Hold each corn cob by its pointed end, steadying the stalk end on a cutting board. Using a sharp knife, cut down along the corn cob to strip off the kernels, turning it with each cut. In a bowl, combine the corn kernels with the tomatoes, bell pepper, celery, onion, and jalapeño chile, tossing to mix well.

In a bowl, whisk together the mayonnaise and yogurt until smooth. Whisk in the chicken stock and vinegar. Pour over the corn mixture. Toss well and season with salt and pepper. Cover and refrigerate for at least 1 hour or for up to 3 hours.

Remove from the refrigerator, transfer to a serving bowl, sprinkle with the cilantro and parsley, and serve.

Serves 6

6 large ears of corn, husks and silk removed

12 cherry tomatoes, or 1 large tomato, chopped

1 large green bell pepper (capsicum), seeded and chopped

1 celery stalk, chopped

1 small red onion, chopped

1 small jalapeño chile, seeded and minced

1/2 cup (4 fl oz/125 ml) mayonnaise

1/4 cup (2 oz/60 g) plain yogurt

1/4 cup (2 fl oz/60 ml) Chicken Stock (page 288) or broth

2 tablespoons red wine vinegar

Salt and freshly ground pepper

2 teaspoons chopped fresh cilantro (fresh coriander)

2 teaspoons chopped fresh flat-leaf (Italian) parsley

Stuffed Poblano Chiles

Once the chiles are filled, you need to cook them for only a few minutes before bringing them piping hot to a table set in the garden or on a deck or patio. You can roast the chiles and toast the nuts ahead of time.

Preheat a broiler (grill). Place the chiles on a broiler pan and broil (grill) about 4 inches (10 cm) from the heat source, turning as necessary, until the skins are evenly blackened and blistered. Remove from the broiler, drape the chiles loosely with aluminum foil, and let stand for 10 minutes, then peel away the skins. Cut a lengthwise slit in each chile, but leave the stem intact. Remove the seeds, being careful not to pierce the flesh. If necessary, rinse the chiles to remove any remaining charred skin, then pat dry. Set aside.

Place a frying pan over medium-high heat and add the pine nuts. Toast, stirring, until lightly browned, 4–5 minutes. Be careful they do not burn. Transfer to a bowl and add the sun-dried tomatoes, ricotta cheese, chopped oregano or marjoram, salt, and pepper. Mix well. Divide the cheese mixture evenly among the chiles, carefully spooning it into the chiles through the slits. Pinch the edges of the slits closed.

In a nonstick frying pan over medium heat, warm the vegetable oil. When the oil is hot, place the filled chiles in the pan and gently press down on them with the back of a wooden spoon or a spatula. Cook just until the cheese begins to soften, 1–2 minutes. Turn, gently press again, and cook until the cheese is thoroughly hot, about 1 minute longer.

Transfer the chiles to a warmed platter and spoon the chopped fresh tomatoes over the tops. Sprinkle with minced oregano or marjoram, if desired. Serve immediately.

Serves 4

4 poblano chiles

1/4 cup (11/4 oz/37 g) pine nuts

12 drained, oil-packed sun-dried tomatoes, minced

1/2 lb (250 g) ricotta cheese

1/4 cup (1/3 oz/10 g) chopped fresh oregano or marjoram

1/2 teaspoon salt

1/2 teaspoon freshly ground pepper

1 teaspoon vegetable oil

3 fresh tomatoes, peeled, seeded, and finely chopped

Minced fresh oregano or marjoram (optional)

Roast Red Potato Salad

The secret to great-tasting potato salad is to dress the potatoes while they are hot, so they will absorb the flavors of the dressing. You can roast these potatoes at any temperature necessary to pair them with meat; though the cooking time will change.

3 lb (1.5 kg) red potatoes

2/3 cup (5 oz/155 g) coarse salt

2 tablespoons dry white wine

2 tablespoons extra-virgin olive oil

3 tablespoons sherry wine vinegar

4 shallots, coarsely chopped

3 tablespoons fresh tarragon leaves

3/4 cup (6 fl oz/180 ml) pure olive oil

2 tablespoons Dijon mustard

Freshly ground pepper

3 green (spring) onions, chopped

1/2 bunch fresh flat-leaf (Italian) parsley, chopped

Preheat the oven to 400°F (200°C).

Scrub the potatoes but do not peel them. Place the potatoes in a baking pan large enough to hold them in a single layer and pour the coarse salt over them. Roast until tender but firm when pierced, 50–60 minutes depending upon the size of the potatoes.

Remove the potatoes from the oven and, using 3 pot holders, rub off the excess salt from each one. Place the potatoes on a cutting board and cut them into narrow slices. (If they are still very hot, hold with a pot holder or paper towel as you slice.) Transfer to a bowl. Immediately drizzle the wine, extra-virgin olive oil, and 1 tablespoon of the vinegar over the hot potatoes. Toss gently and set aside.

In a food processor, combine the shallots and tarragon and process to chop finely. Add to the potatoes and toss gently.

In a small bowl, whisk together the pure olive oil, the remaining 2 tablespoons vinegar, and the mustard. Season with pepper to taste. Pour the mustard mixture over the potatoes, cover with plastic wrap, and refrigerate for at least 1 hour or up to 2 days.

Remove the potato salad from the refrigerator. Add the green onions and parsley and toss gently. Taste and adjust the seasonings. If desired, let stand for about 1 hour before serving. Transfer to a bowl and serve.

Serves 8

Bourbon Baked Beans

Baked beans have a long history in the United States. In this version, bourbon gives the finished beans their distinctive flavor. This side dish is delicious when paired with grilled chicken or Chilied Flank Steak (page 108).

Pick over the beans and discard any misshapen beans or stones. Rinse the beans and drain, then place in a large pot and add water to cover by 2 inches (5 cm). Bring the water to a boil and boil for 2 minutes. Remove from the heat, cover, and let the beans stand for 1 hour. Drain.

Preheat the oven to 300°F (150°C). Butter a Dutch oven and rub the surface with the garlic clove. Then, mince the garlic and set aside.

Chop 3 of the bacon slices. In a large pot over medium heat, sauté the chopped bacon until crisp, 3–4 minutes. Add the onion and sauté until just beginning to soften, about 1 minute. Add the reserved minced garlic and sauté until the onion and garlic are lightly browned, about 4 minutes longer. Stir in 1/2 cup (4 fl oz/ 125 ml) of the beef stock, the bourbon, chili sauce, molasses, Worcestershire sauce, brown sugar, mustard, curry powder, pepper, and paprika. Mix well, stir in the drained beans, and transfer to the garlic-rubbed pot. Lay the remaining 3 slices of the bacon evenly over the top.

Cover the pot and bake for 2 hours. Reduce the oven temperature to 275°F (135°C) and continue to bake, adding the remaining 1 cup (8 fl oz/250 ml) stock as needed to keep the beans from drying out, until they are tender, about 1 1/2 hours longer. Uncover and cut the bacon—which will have shrunk quite a bit—into pieces with scissors. Serve the beans hot.

Serves 6

2 1/4 cups (1 lb/500 g) dried Great Northern or other large white beans

1 clove garlic, lightly crushed

6 slices thick-cut bacon

1 large yellow onion, finely chopped

1 1/2 cups (12 fl oz/375 ml) Beef Stock (page 288) or broth

1/2 cup (4 fl oz/125 ml) bourbon whiskey

5 tablespoons (2 1/2 fl oz/75 ml) bottled chili sauce

1/4 cup (2 1/2 oz/75 g) molasses

2 teaspoons Worcestershire sauce

2 tablespoons dark brown sugar

1 tablespoon dry mustard

1 teaspoon curry powder

1/2 teaspoon freshly ground pepper

1/4 teaspoon Hungarian hot paprika

Oven-Roasted Potato Pancake

This crispy pancake, with its soft, tender interior, will bring accolades from everyone at the dinner table. Try it with chicken or lamb dishes such as Roast Chicken with Garlic and Herb (page 69) or Mint and Chive–Marinated Leg of Lamb (page 133).

3–4 tablespoons olive oil

4 or 5 large baking potatoes

2 teaspoons coarse salt, or more as needed

Freshly ground pepper

1/4 teaspoon Hungarian sweet paprika, or as needed

1/2 bunch fresh flat-leaf (Italian) parsley, stems discarded and leaves chopped

Preheat the oven to 425°F (220°C). Oil a ceramic 11-inch (28-cm) quiche dish or a glass 10-inch (25-cm) pie dish with 1 teaspoon of the olive oil.

Shred the potatoes into a bowl, working as quickly as possible to prevent them from turning brown. Transfer the shredded potatoes, a few handfuls at a time, to the prepared dish. Sprinkle each batch with some of the coarse salt, a few grindings of pepper, and a few drops of olive oil. Repeat the layering until the potatoes are level with the rim of the dish. Drizzle the top with the remaining olive oil, then season with salt, pepper, and the paprika.

Roast until the potatoes are dark brown and crisp on top yet soft inside when pierced with a fork, 50–55 minutes. If the potatoes begin to brown too quickly, reduce the oven temperature to 350°F (180°C).

Remove the potato pancake from the oven and let rest for 5–10 minutes, then cut into wedges. Sprinkle with the parsley and serve immediately.

Serves 6

Double Corn–Chile Spoon Bread

Light, fluffy spoon bread, reminiscent of a soufflé, is laced with cheese, corn kernels, and green chiles to make a complete meal when accompanied with a platter of sliced tomatoes and a green salad.

Preheat a broiler (grill). Place the chiles on a broiler pan and place under the broiler. Broil (grill), turning as needed, just until the skins are evenly blackened and blistered. Transfer the chiles to a plate, drape with aluminum foil, and let stand for 10 minutes. Peel away the skins, then cut the chiles in half lengthwise and remove and discard the seeds.

Preheat the oven to 350°F (180°C).

In a frying pan over medium heat, cook the bacon until barely browned, 6–7 minutes. Transfer to paper towels to drain.

Butter an 8-inch (20-cm) square baking dish. Layer the chiles in the bottom of the prepared dish. Sprinkle evenly with the jack and cheddar cheeses. In a bowl, beat the egg whites with an electric mixer until fluffy but not stiff. In another, larger bowl, combine the egg yolks, corn kernels, milk, sour cream, cornmeal, flour, and salt. Using a fork, beat until blended. Using a rubber spatula, gently fold the egg whites into the cornmeal mixture. Spoon the egg mixture evenly over the cheese and chiles. Scatter the bacon pieces over the top.

Bake the spoon bread until it is set around the sides but still jiggles slightly in the center when the pan is gently shaken, about 20 minutes. Scoop from the dish to serve. Serve immediately.

Serves 4–6

6 large Anaheim or other mild green chiles

2 bacon slices, cut into 1-inch (2.5-cm) pieces

1/2 cup (2 oz/60 g) shredded Monterey jack cheese

1/2 cup (2 oz/60 g) shredded sharp Cheddar cheese

3 eggs, separated

Kernels from 3 ears white or yellow corn

1/3 cup (3 fl oz/80 ml) milk

2 tablespoons sour cream

2 tablespoons fine yellow cornmeal

2 tablespoons all-purpose (plain) flour

1/2 teaspoon salt

Acorn Squash Stuffed with Wild Rice

½ cup (3 oz/90 g) wild rice

1 teaspoon coarse salt, plus more salt as needed

10 dried shiitake mushrooms, soaked in warm water to cover for 30 minutes

3 large acorn squash, 2–2½ lb (1–1.25 kg) each, halved lengthwise and seeds and fibers discarded

1 tablespoon maple syrup

2 tablespoons unsalted butter

1 tablespoon olive oil, or as needed

1 yellow onion, finely diced

1 celery stalk, finely diced

1 carrot, peeled and finely diced

1 tablespoon minced fresh marjoram, or 1 teaspoon dried marjoram

Freshly ground pepper

1 tablespoon Madeira wine, or as needed

½ cup (2 oz/60 g) pecan halves

In a saucepan over high heat, combine the wild rice, 4 cups (32 fl oz/1 l) water, and 1 teaspoon salt. Bring to a boil, reduce the heat to low, cover partially, and simmer until tender, about 45 minutes. Drain and set aside.

Meanwhile, drain the shiitake mushrooms, reserving the liquid. Squeeze all the liquid from the mushrooms and pat them dry with paper towels. Remove the tough stems and cut the caps into slivers. Set aside.

Preheat the oven to 400°F (200°C). Oil a roasting pan. Place the squash halves, cut sides down, in the pan. Roast until the edges are soft but the centers are firm, about 35 minutes. While the squash is roasting, in a large frying pan over medium-low heat, melt the butter with 1 tablespoon olive oil. Add the onion, celery, and carrot and cook, stirring often, until the onion is translucent and the other vegetables are tender-crisp, about 12 minutes. Season with the marjoram, and coarse salt and pepper to taste. Stir in the mushrooms and sauté for 1 minute. Add the Madeira and cook until it is absorbed, about 2 minutes. If the mixture is dry, add a few more drops olive oil, then stir in the cooked wild rice. Adjust the seasonings.

Remove the squash from the oven, turn cut-sides up, and spoon ½ teaspoon maple syrup into each cavity. Divide the stuffing into the squash halves. Drizzle about 1 tablespoon of the reserved mushroom liquid over each half. Return the squash to the oven and continue to roast until the squash is tender when pierced with a fork, about 30 minutes longer. If the stuffing is browning too fast or drying out, reduce the oven temperature to 350°F (180°C) or loosely tent with aluminum foil.

Meanwhile, in a dry frying pan over high heat toast the pecans, shaking the pan constantly, until the nuts begin to darken, 3–4 minutes. Transfer the squash halves to warmed individual plates and sprinkle the pecans on top. Serve immediately.

Serves 6

Grilled Summer Squash with Green Sauce

Zucchini (courgettes) are one of the most popular vegetables for grilling. It's easy to prepare, to cook quickly and is delicious, particularly when served with this tasty green sauce. Serve this summer side dish with grilled fish or chicken.

To make the green sauce, in a food processor, combine the olive oil, lemon juice, shallot, capers, anchovies, white pepper, and the parsley. Process until smooth. Transfer to a bowl and stir in the chopped basil. Cover and refrigerate until ready to serve.

Cut the zucchini lengthwise into $1/2$ inch slices. Place in a large, shallow nonaluminum dish. In a small bowl, mash together the garlic and 2 tablespoons of the olive oil with the back of a spoon until smooth. Whisk in the remaining 4 tablespoons (2 fl oz/60 ml) oil, the thyme, salt, and black pepper. Pour over the zucchini. Cover and let stand at room temperature for 30 minutes.

Prepare a hot fire for direct-heat cooking in a grill (see pages 8–9). Position the grill rack 4–6 inches (10–15 cm) above the fire.

Place the zucchini on the grill rack. Cook, turning once, until just tender, 4–5 minutes on each side. Transfer to a serving dish and spoon the green sauce evenly over the top. Serve immediately.

Serves 4

FOR THE GREEN SAUCE:

1/2 cup (4 fl oz/125 ml) olive oil

1/4 cup (2 fl oz/60 ml) lemon juice

1 shallot, chopped

2 teaspoons capers

2 anchovy fillets in olive oil

1/2 teaspoon ground white pepper

1/2 cup (3/4 oz/20 g) coarsely chopped fresh flat-leaf (Italian) parsley

1/4 cup (1/3 oz/10 g) chopped fresh basil

4 or 5 small zucchini (courgettes) or yellow summer squash, about 1 lb (500 g)

4 cloves garlic, minced

6 tablespoons (3 fl oz/90 ml) olive oil

1 tablespoon chopped fresh thyme

1/2 teaspoon salt

1/2 teaspoon freshly ground black pepper

Potato and Roasted Garlic Gratin

You don't need to peel the potatoes for this quick and hearty baked side dish. There is a wealth of minerals contained in their skins, and the skins also add a pleasing rustic texture to the finished dish.

1 large head garlic, about 2 oz (60 g)

2 cups (16 fl oz/500 ml) Vegetable Stock (page 288) or broth

2 lb (1 kg) russet potatoes, unpeeled, thinly sliced

1 large yellow onion, thinly sliced

1 tablespoon chopped fresh sage

Salt and freshly ground pepper

¼ cup (1 oz/30 g) grated Parmesan cheese

3 tablespoons fresh bread crumbs

Preheat the oven to 300°F (150°C).

Wrap the unpeeled whole garlic head in aluminum foil. Bake until the cloves are very soft, about 1½ hours. Remove from the oven and set aside. Raise the oven temperature to 350°F (180°C).

Squeeze the pulp from the garlic cloves into a large bowl. Gradually whisk in the stock or broth. Add the potatoes, onion, and sage and toss to coat the potato slices evenly. Press half of the potato mixture into a 7-by-11-inch (18-by-28-cm) baking dish, forming an even layer. Season generously with salt and pepper and sprinkle with 1 tablespoon of the cheese. Top with the remaining potato mixture, and press it into an even layer. Pour the liquid mixture remaining in the bowl evenly over the top. Cover the dish with aluminum foil and bake for 1 hour.

In a small bowl, stir together the remaining 3 tablespoons cheese and the bread crumbs. Uncover the baking dish and sprinkle the cheese mixture evenly over the top. Continue to bake, uncovered, until the potatoes are tender and crusty, about 50 minutes.

Remove the dish from the oven, let stand for 10 minutes, and serve.

Serves 8

Tangy Mango Relish

This easy, fresh fruit salsa is a versitile component to any meal. Use it as a condiment for grilled pork, poultry or fish, or as a lively salad for a Southeast Asian-style meal. The juice of the mango is just the right tonic for spicy dishes.

Place the chiles and $1/4$ cup (2 fl oz/60 ml) water in a food processor or blender and process until coarsely puréed, leaving small bits of chile. Transfer to a small saucepan and add the vinegar, sugar, and salt. Cook over medium heat, stirring occasionally, until the sugar dissolves, about 3 minutes. Let cool.

Add the mango, lime juice, mint, and cilantro and stir gently to combine. Cover and let stand at room temperature until the flavors meld, about 20 minutes, before serving.

Serves 8

2 red jalapeño chiles, seeded

3 tablespoons white vinegar

4 teaspoons sugar

$1/2$ teaspoon salt

1 large firm mango, peeled and cut into $3/4$-inch (2-cm) cubes

1 tablespoon lime juice

1 tablespoon coarsely chopped fresh mint

1 tablespoon coarsely chopped fresh cilantro (fresh coriander)

Corn Bread with Chorizo

This flavor-laced corn bread is the perfect partner for many grilled foods, from brisket to ribs. The recipe calls for a bottled chunky-style tomato salsa, but if you have homemade salsa on hand, you can use it instead.

4 chorizo sausages, about 10 oz (315 g) total weight

1 teaspoon plus 2 tablespoons olive oil

6 green (spring) onions, white parts and tender green tops chopped separately

1 red bell pepper (capsicum), seeded and chopped

1 cup (5 oz/155 g) yellow cornmeal

1/3 cup (2 oz/60 g) all-purpose (plain) flour

1 teaspoon baking powder

1 teaspoon sugar

1/2 teaspoon baking soda (bicarbonate of soda)

1/2 teaspoon salt

2 eggs

3/4 cup (6 oz/185 g) plain yogurt

1/2 cup (4 fl oz/125 ml) bottled medium, chunky-style salsa

2/3 cup (5 fl oz/160 ml) milk

1/4 lb (125 g) Monterey jack cheese, shredded

Preheat the oven to 350°F (180°C).

Chop the chorizo. In a 10-inch (25-cm) cast-iron or other ovenproof frying pan over medium-low heat, warm the 1 teaspoon olive oil until hot. Add the chorizo and sauté, stirring occasionally, until the meat is lightly browned and all the fat has been rendered, about 8 minutes. Using a slotted spoon, transfer the sausage to a plate.

Pour off all but 1 tablespoon fat from the pan and return to medium-low heat. Add the white parts of the green onions and sauté until lightly browned, about 4 minutes. Return the chorizo to the pan and stir in the bell pepper. Cover and cook, stirring occasionally, until the pepper begins to soften, about 4 minutes. Uncover and remove from the heat.

In a bowl, stir together the cornmeal, flour, baking powder, sugar, baking soda, and salt. In another large bowl, whisk together the eggs, yogurt, and 2 tablespoons olive oil until smooth. Add the salsa and green onion tops and then stir in the cornmeal mixture in 3 batches, alternating with the milk and ending with the cornmeal. Stir in the cheese and the chorizo mixture. Immediately pour the batter into the frying pan (do not wipe out the pan) and smooth the top.

Bake until golden and firm to the touch, about 40 minutes. Remove from the oven and let stand for at least 15 minutes before serving. Cut into wedges and serve directly from the pan.

Serves 8

Midwestern Coleslaw

This vinegar-based coleslaw is the ideal partner for a mayonnaise-dressed potato salad. Green cabbage can be used, but be sure to substitute red bell pepper for the green. A sprinkling of crumbled fried bacon makes a wonderful garnish.

Combine the cabbage, carrot, bell pepper, and onion in a large bowl. Toss to mix.

In a small saucepan over medium-high heat, stir together the vinegar, sugar, celery seeds, and dry mustard. Bring to a boil, stirring frequently, and then continue to boil, stirring occasionally, until thick, about 15 minutes. Remove from the heat and whisk in $1/4$ cup (2 fl oz/60 ml) water. Immediately pour over the cabbage mixture. Toss well, cover, and refrigerate for 6–8 hours.

Just before serving, remove the coleslaw from the refrigerator and drain off and discard the liquid. (There will be quite a lot of liquid.) Transfer to a serving bowl, sprinkle with the parsley, and serve.

Serves 6

1 small head red cabbage, about 1 lb (500 g), cored and shredded or chopped

1 large carrot, peeled and grated

$1/2$ green bell pepper (capsicum), seeded and minced

1 small white onion, finely chopped

1 cup (8 fl oz/250 ml) cider vinegar

$2/3$ cup (5 oz/155 g) sugar

$1/2$ teaspoon celery seeds

$1/2$ teaspoon dry mustard

1 tablespoon chopped fresh parsley

Ratatouille on the Grill

2 small eggplants (aubergines), about 1 lb (500 g) total weight

Salt

1 large Vidalia or other sweet onion, unpeeled, soaked in water for 30 minutes

1 large green bell pepper (capsicum)

1 large red bell pepper (capsicum)

2 firm but ripe tomatoes, halved crosswise

About $1/4$ cup (2 fl oz/60 ml) olive oil

2 yellow summer squashes, cut lengthwise into slices $1/4$ inch (6 mm) thick

1 clove garlic, minced

$1/2$ teaspoon chopped fresh thyme

$1/2$ teaspoon red pepper flakes

1 tablespoon chopped fresh dill, plus sprigs for garnish (optional)

Cut the eggplants lengthwise into $1/4$ inch (6 mm) slices. Sprinkle generously with salt and place in a colander. Let stand for 30 minutes to drain the liquid.

Prepare a hot fire for direct-heat cooking in a charcoal grill (see pages 8–9). Position the grill rack 4–6 inches (10–15 cm) above the fire. When the coals are covered with white ash, drain the onion and place it directly in the hot coals, making sure it is well covered. Cook until easily pierced with a sharp knife, about 30 minutes. Using long-handled tongs, remove the onion from the coals and let cool.

Meanwhile, brush the eggplant slices, whole peppers, and tomato halves with about 2 teaspoons of the olive oil. Place the eggplant around the edges of the rack and the peppers and the tomato halves, cut sides down, in the center. Cover the grill and open the vents. Cook, turning occasionally, until the eggplant and tomatoes are tender and the peppers are well charred on all sides, about 10 minutes for the tomatoes and eggplant, and 25 minutes for the peppers. Transfer the vegetables to a cutting board when ready. Drape the peppers with aluminum foil and let stand for about 10 minutes, then peel away the skin. Remove the stems, seeds, and ribs, then cut lengthwise into strips $1/4$ inch (6 mm) wide. Cut each strip in half crosswise.

Brush the squash slices with about $1/2$ teaspoon oil. While other vegetables are cooling, grill the squash, turning once, until tender, about 10 minutes total.

Peel the onion and cut it in half. Cut each half into slices $1/4$ inch (6 mm) thick. Transfer to a large bowl. Coarsely chop the tomatoes and squash. Cut the eggplant crosswise into narrow strips. Add to the onion along with the pepper strips. Add 3 tablespoons olive oil and the garlic, thyme, and red pepper flakes. Toss lightly to mix. Season with salt and toss again. Sprinkle with the chopped dill and garnish with dill sprigs, if desired. Serve warm or at room temperature.

Serves 4

Basic Recipes

The following basic recipes are used throughout the book. Once you have mastered them, you can turn to them often, as delicious kitchen staples. Use the freshest ingredients that you can find.

Chicken Stock

Any type of chicken can be used for making this stock, although pieces of a stewing chicken (usually a more mature bird) will yield the most flavor.

2¹/₂ lb (1.25 kg) chicken pieces, including bones

4 celery stalks with leaves, coarsely chopped

2 carrots, peeled and coarsely chopped

2 yellow onions, coarsely chopped

2 leeks, white part only, carefully washed and coarsely chopped

Bouquet Garni (page 290)

Put the chicken in a large stockpot and add cold water to cover by 2 inches. Bring to a gentle boil over medium-high heat. Reduce the heat to low and simmer for 30 minutes. While the stock simmers, using a large spoon, skim off any scum that forms on the surface.

Add the celery, carrots, onions, leeks, and bouquet garni. Cover partially and boil gently for 30 minutes longer; check periodically, skimming off any scum that forms on the surface.

Remove from the heat and remove the solids with a slotted spoon or skimmer. Strain the stock through a fine-mesh sieve lined with cheesecloth (muslin) into a clean pot (if using the stock immediately) or storage container (if saving the stock for future use). If using the stock immediately, use a large spoon to skim the fat from the surface of the stock. Discard the fat and use the stock in the desired recipe.

If storing the stock, let it cool to room temperature, then cover tightly and refrigerate for up to 5 days, or freeze for up to 6 months. Before using the stock, remove the solidified fat that sits on top of the stock.

Makes about 5 cups (40 fl oz/1.25 l)

Vegetable Stock

Sautéing the vegetables before adding water gives this particular stock a special depth of flavor.

2 tablespoons vegetable oil

2 large sweet onions, coarsely chopped

4 celery stalks with leaves, coarsely chopped

3 carrots, peeled and coarsely chopped

1 green bell pepper (capsicum), seeded, deribbed, and coarsely chopped

1 teaspoon salt

Bouquet Garni (page 290)

In a large stockpot over medium heat, warm the vegetable oil. Add the onions, celery, carrots, and bell pepper and sauté, stirring often, until the onions are translucent, about 10 minutes. Add 10 cups (2¹/₂ qt/2.5 l) water, the salt, and the bouquet garni. Bring to a gentle boil over medium-high heat. Reduce the heat to low and simmer for 30 minutes.

Remove the stock from the heat and lift out the solids with a slotted spoon. Strain the stock through a fine-mesh sieve lined with cheesecloth (muslin) into a clean pot (if using the stock immediately) or storage container (if saving the stock for future use).

If using the stock immediately, proceed with the desired recipe as directed. If storing the stock, let it cool to room temperature, then cover tightly and refrigerate for up to 5 days, or freeze for up to 12 months.

Makes about 8 cups (64 fl oz/2 l)

Beef Stock

Making stock at home is an all-day task, but the results are well worth the time. You can prepare a large batch of stock and freeze it in small containers for future use.

6 lb (3 kg) meaty beef shanks

Beef scraps or other trimmings, if available

2 onions, coarsely chopped

1 leek, trimmed, carefully washed, and coarsely chopped

2 carrots, peeled and coarsely chopped

1 celery stalk, coarsely chopped

Mushroom stems (optional)

6 cloves garlic

4 fresh parsley sprigs

10 whole peppercorns

3 fresh thyme sprigs

2 small bay leaves

Preheat the oven to 450°F (220°C). Place the beef shanks in a large roasting pan and roast, turning occasionally, until browned but not burned, about 1 1/2 hours.

Transfer the browned shanks to a large stockpot, reserving the juices in the pan, and add cold water to cover by 2 inches. Add the beef scraps, if using. Bring to a boil over medium-high heat. Reduce the heat to low and simmer, uncovered, for 2 hours. While the stock simmers, using a large spoon, skim off any scum that forms on the surface. Add water as needed to keep the bones generously immersed.

Meanwhile, place the roasting pan on the stove top. Add the onions, leek, carrots, and celery to the fat remaining in the pan. Brown over high heat, stirring often, until the vegetables caramelize but are not scorched, 15–20 minutes.

When the shanks have simmered for 2 hours, add the browned vegetables to the stockpot. Pour 1 cup (8 fl oz/250 ml) hot water into the roasting pan, bring to a simmer, and deglaze the pan by stirring to dislodge any browned bits from the bottom. Add these juices to the stockpot.

Place the mushroom stems (if using), garlic, parsley, peppercorns, thyme, and bay leaves on a square of cheesecloth (muslin) and tie with kitchen string into a small bag. Add to the stockpot. Simmer over low heat, uncovered, for 6 hours longer (for a total of 8 hours).

Remove from the heat and remove the solids with a slotted spoon or skimmer. Strain the stock through a fine-mesh sieve lined with cheesecloth (muslin) into a clean pot (if using the stock immediately) or into a storage container (if saving the stock for future use). If using the stock, use a large spoon to skim the fat from the surface of the stock. Discard the skimmed fat and use the stock as directed in the desired recipe.

If storing the stock, let it cool to room temperature, then cover tightly and refrigerate for up to 5 days, or freeze for up to 6 months. Before using the stock, remove the solidified fat that sits on top of the stock.

Makes 4–5 qt (4–5 l)

Veal Stock

6 lb (3 kg) meaty veal shanks

Veal scraps or other trimmings, if available

2 onions, coarsely chopped

1 leek, trimmed, carefully washed, and coarsely chopped

2 carrots, peeled and coarsely chopped

1 celery stalk, coarsely chopped

Mushroom stems (optional)

6 cloves garlic

4 fresh parsley sprigs

10 whole peppercorns

3 fresh thyme sprigs

2 small bay leaves

Preheat the oven to 450°F (220°C). Place the veal shanks in a large roasting pan and roast, turning occasionally, until browned but not burned, about 1 1/2 hours.

Transfer the browned shanks to a large stockpot, reserving the juices in the pan, and add cold water to cover by 2 inches. Add the veal scraps, if using. Bring to a boil over medium-high heat. Reduce the heat to low and simmer, uncovered, for 2 hours. While the stock simmers, using a large spoon, skim off any scum that forms on the surface. Add water as needed to keep the bones generously immersed.

Meanwhile, place the roasting pan on the stove top. Add the onions, leek, carrots, and celery to the fat remaining in the pan. Brown over high heat, stirring often, until the vegetables caramelize but are not scorched, 15–20 minutes.

When the shanks have simmered for 2 hours, add the browned vegetables to the stockpot. Pour 1 cup (8 fl oz/ 250 ml) hot water into the roasting pan, bring to a simmer, and deglaze the pan by stirring to dislodge any browned bits from the bottom. Add these juices to the stockpot.

Place the mushroom stems (if using), garlic, parsley, peppercorns, thyme, and bay leaves on a square of cheesecloth (muslin) and tie with kitchen string into a small bag. Add to the stockpot. Simmer over low heat, uncovered, for 6 hours longer (for a total of 8 hours).

Remove the stock from the heat and lift out the solids with a slotted spoon or skimmer. Strain the stock through a fine-mesh sieve lined with cheesecloth (muslin) into a large clean pot (if using the stock) or storage container (if saving the stock for future use). If using the stock immediately, use a large spoon to skim the excess fat from the surface of the stock. Discard the skimmed fat and use the stock in the desired recipe.

If storing the stock, let it cool to room temperature, then cover tightly and refrigerate for up to 5 days, or freeze for up to 6 months. Before using the stock, remove the solidified fat that sits on top of the stock.

Makes 4–5 qt (4–5 l)

Bouquet Garni

6 whole peppercorns

1 bay leaf

1 clove garlic, sliced

3 fresh parsley sprigs

Csing kitchen shears cut out a 6-inch (15-cm) square of cheesecloth (muslin). Place the peppercorns, bay leaf, garlic, and parsley sprigs on the center of the cheesecloth, bring the corners together,

and tie securely with kitchen string. Use as directed in individual recipes.

Makes 1 sachet

Seasoning Rub

An all-purpose spice blend is one of the secrets to successful grilling and roasting. Rubbed onto meats, this mixture provides an abundance of flavor. Try toasting the spices before mixing them together.

2 cloves garlic, minced

1½ teaspoons paprika

1 teaspoon salt

1 teaspoon cayenne pepper

½ teaspoon ground black pepper

In a small bowl, stir together the garlic, paprika, salt, cayenne pepper, and black pepper. Rub the mixture onto both sides of the meat and coat evenly.

Makes about ½ cup (1½ oz/45 G)

Asian Dressing

2 tablespoons peanut oil

3 cloves garlic, finely minced

1 piece fresh ginger, about 1 inch (2.5 cm) long, peeled and grated

2 green (spring) onions, including tender green tops, minced

¼ cup (2 fl oz/60 ml) dark soy sauce or Japanese soy sauce

3 tablespoons red wine vinegar or balsamic vinegar

1½ tablespoons Asian sesame oil

1 teaspoon hot chili oil, or to taste

1 teaspoon sugar

½ teaspoon salt

In a small saucepan over medium heat, combine the peanut oil, garlic, and ginger. Sauté, without browning, until aromatic, about 1 minute.

Remove from the heat, add the green onions, soy sauce, vinegar, sesame oil, chili oil, sugar, and salt and stir to combine.

Set aside for the flavors to blend and mix well before using.

Makes about ½ cup (4 fl oz/125 ml)

Garlic-Lime Dipping Sauce

¼ cup (2 oz/60 g) sugar

¼ cup (2 fl oz/60 ml) hot water

1 red Serrano chile

2 cloves garlic, chopped

⅓ cup (3 fl oz/80 ml) limejuice

¼ cup (2 fl oz/60 ml) fish sauce

In a medium bow, combine the sugar and hot water, stirring to dissolve the sugar. Seed and finely chop the Serrano chile. Add to the sauce with the garlic, lime juice, and fish sauce.

Makes about ¾ cup (6 fl oz/180 ml)

Grill Tempertures

If you do not have a grill thermometer, you can estimate the temperature of a charcoal grill with a simple hand test (gas grills will come with a built-in temperature gauge). Hold your hand, palm down, 4 inches (10 cm) above the fire and count the seconds before you need to pull your hand away.

HEAT LEVEL	TEMPERATURE	HAND TEST
Very high	450°F (230°C) and higher	Less than 1 second
High	400°–450°F (200°–230°C)	1 or 2 seconds
Medium-high	375°–400°F (190°–200°C)	2 or 3 seconds
Medium	350°–375°F (180°–190°C)	3 or 4 seconds
Medium-low	325°–350°F (165°–180°C)	4 or 5 seconds
Low	300°–325°F (150°–165°C)	5 seconds or more

Doneness Temperatures

The temperatures listed below are taken before the resting period (see page 10); they will rise 5°–10°F (3°–6°C) during this time to reach the optimum level of doneness.

ITEM	RARE	MEDIUM–RARE	MEDIUM	MEDIUM–WELL	WELL
Beef	130°F (54°C)	140°F (60°C)	145°F (63°C)	150°F (65°C)	160°F (71°C) or more
Chicken					170°F (76°C)
Pork			145°–150°F (62°–65°C)	150°–160°F (65°C–71°C)	160°F (71°C) or more
Duck					175°F (79°C)

Glossary

Acorn Squash About 6 inches in diameter, this squash has a dark green, ribbed shell and orange flesh

Anchovy Indigenous to the Mediterranean and Atlantic coastlines of Spain and Portugal, anchovies are used widely in the cuisines of those specific countries, as well as in Italy and southern France. They are generally packed in oil and are drained or rinsed before using.

Artichoke This vegetable is actually the flower bud harvested from a plant of the thistle family. Baby artichokes are not immature artichokes, but simply small ones that grow lower on the plant. All the artichokes have a mild, nutty flavor and should be heavy for their size, with closed leaves.

Arugula Also known as rocket, these slender, green, deeply notched leaves have a nutty, slightly peppery taste. Larger leaves will be more pungent then smaller ones.

Asparagus These tall, tender-crisp spears can be as thin as a pencil or as thick as your thumb. Look for firm stalks and tightly closed tips.

Avocado Rich in flavor and texture, avocados are most commonly available in two varieties: the dark green, dimpled Hass and the smoother, paler green Fuerte. Hass avocados boast the highest oil content and will produce the best results in guacamole.

Baby Back Ribs Pork ribs taken from the center section of the loin. They are smaller, less meaty, and less fatty than spare ribs.

Banana Leaves Used in Mexican, Caribbean, and Southeast Asian cooking, these large leaves impart a subtle flavor to foods wrapped in them for grilling or steaming. They are available fresh or frozen in specialty markets.

Beets This hardy root vegetable often boasts a deep, rich red color combined with a sweet, earthy flavor. Fresh beets should have the greens attached and 1 to 2 inches (2.5 to 5 cm) of the root ends.

Belgian Endive These pale, furled, shoots are also known as witloof or chicory. Although most endives are creamy white with just a touch of yellowish green at the edges, a variety with pale burgundy tips is also available.

Bok Choy The Asian green bok choy has a flavor somewhere between celery and cabbage. Give particular attention to rinsing, as grit is usually lodged between the stems.

Broth & Stock Commercially produced, well-flavored liquids made by cooking meat, poultry, fish, or vegetables in water. Canned broths tend to be saltier than homemade, so seek out high-quality "reduced-sodium" products for better control of the seasoning in your dish. You can also purchase excellent "homemade" stocks fresh or frozen from upscale supermarkets and specialty-food stores.

Buttermilk Made by adding bacteria to skimmed milk to convert sugars to acid, buttermilk is slightly thick and tangy. It adds tenderness and flavor to baked goods.

Capers The unopened flower buds of bushes native to the Mediterranean, capers are dried, cured, and then usually packed in a vinegar brine. Rinse them briefly and blot dry before using.

Chiles Fresh chiles range in size from tiny to large, and in heat intensity from mild to fiery hot. To reduce the heat of a chile, remove the ribs and seeds. When working with hot chiles, wear latex gloves to avoid burning your skin, then wash your hands and any utensils thoroughly with hot, soapy water the moment you finish.
Arbol Chili About 3 inches long, narrow, and very hot. These chiles are

bright orange when fresh and red to orange when dried.

Chipotle A dried and smoked jalapeño chile, with lots of flavor and lots of heat. These dark brown chiles about 3 inches (7.5 cm) long are sold either dried whole, ground, or packed in an onion-y tomato mixture called adobo sauce.

Hungarian A small, sweet, bright red, round chile measuring about 2 inches or less in diameter. This pleasant-tasting chile does not pack much punch and is often pickled.

Jalapeño This fresh hot chile measures 2–4 inches (5–10 cm) long, has a generous amount of flesh, and ranges from mildly hot to fiery. Green jalapeños are widely available in supermarkets.

Poblano Large and fairly mild, the fresh, dark green poblano is about 5 inches (13 cm) long and has broad "shoulders." Poblanos, which are usually roasted and peeled, have a nutty flavor and are often stuffed for chile rellenos.

Serrano Similar to jalapeños in heat intensity, the serrano is sleeker and tends to have more consistent heat. Although they are most often available fresh, occasionally you may find dried *serranos secos*.

Chile Powder A pure powder made by grinding a single specific variety of dried chile. Ancho and New Mexico chile powders are the most common. Seek out chipotle chile powder for a

Cheeses

Visiting a good cheese shop is a rewarding experience, since you'll be able to taste a variety of types before you buy. Store cheeses in a warmer part of the refrigerator, such as the door, wrapped in parchment (baking) or waxed paper rather than plastic, to allow them to breathe.

Blue Cheese that is inoculated with spores of special molds to develop a fine network of blue veins for a strong, sharp, peppery flavor and a crumbly texture.

Fontina A mild, fruity Italian cow's milk cheese with a pleasing firmness and a light but heady aroma.

Feta A young cheese sometimes made with goat's milk but more traditionally made from sheep's milk, feta is known for its unique, crumbly texture. Feta's saltiness is heightened by the brine in which the cheese is packed.

Goat Made from pure goat's milk, or a blend of goat's and cows's milk, fresh goat cheese is creamy and tangy. Montrachet, a well-know variety is soft and spreadable.

Manchego A Spanish sheep's milk cheese with a mild, pale yellow interior dotted with holes and tasting mild and a little salty

Monterey Jack A soft, white, mild cow's milk cheese that originated in California, either with tiny "eyes" or smooth depending on where it was made. Jack is often sold infused with hot red chiles and called "pepper jack".

Mozzerella A mild, creamy cheese made from cow's or water buffalo's milk curd formed into balls. If possible, seek out fresh mozzarella, which is sold surrounded by a little of the whey, rather than the rubbery products made in large factories.

Parmesan This firm, aged, salty cheese is made from partially skimmed cow's milk. Seek out imported Parmigiano-Reggiano, which has a rich, nutty flavor and a pleasant, granular texture; it is the most renowned of all Parmesan cheeses.

Ricotta A whey based cheese made by heating the whey left over from making sheep's, goat's, or cow's milk cheeses. Most Italian ricotta is made from sheep's milk. It takes no solid shape but is sold in plastic containers. Fresh Italian ricotta is superb.

Roquefort A sheep's milk cheese from France with a moist, crumbly interior and true, clean, strong flavor. Some Roqueforts can be rather salty.

particularly smoky flavor. Do not confuse chile powder with chili powder, typically a blend of powdered dried chile, oregano, cumin, and other seasonings.

Chili Sauce Not to be confused with Asian chile sauces, this American-style sauce is a mild ketchuplike blend of tomatoes, chili powder, onions, green bell peppers (capsicums), vinegar, sugar, and spices. Look for it near the condiments in the supermarket.

Chorizo Coarsely ground spicy pork sausage used in Mexican and Spanish cooking. It's best to remove the casings before cooking.

Coconut Milk Rich, nutty-flavored, coconut milk, made by soaking grated coconut in water, is an essential ingredient throughout the tropics. It thickens sauces, turns rice dishes creamy, flavors desserts, smooths out soups, and is perfect foil for the heat of chiles. Coconut milk should not be confused with canned sweetened coconut cream, sometimes labeled "cream of coconut," which is used primarily for desserts and tropical drinks.

Cucumber, English Also called hothouse cucumbers, these cucumbers can grow up to 2 feet (60 cm) long. They are nearly seedless, which makes them a popular choice for soups and salads.

Curry Powder This ground spice blend can include turmeric, cumin, coriander, pepper, cardamom, mustard, cloves, and ginger. Madras curry powder is a version with medium heat.

Eggplant The familiar globe eggplant (aubergine) is usually large, egg or pear shaped, with a skin that looks almost black.

Fig, Black Mission Small and sweet, Black Mission figs are one of more that 150 fig varieties. When ripe, they have a deep purple-black color and should feel soft when gently pressed.

Fish Sauce A clear liquid used in southeast Asian cooking and as a table condiment, much like soy sauce. It ranges in color from amber to dark brown and has a pungent aroma and strong salty flavor.

Garlic When buying garlic, choose plump, firm heads with no brown discoloration. (A tinge of purple is fine, even desirable.) Always take care not to cook garlic beyond a light gold, or it can taste harsh and bitter.

Ginger A refreshing combination of spicy and sweet in both aroma and flavor, ginger adds a lively note to many recipes, particularly Asian

dishes. Select ginger that is firm and heavy and has a smooth skin.

Haricot Vert Also called French green bean or fillet bean. Haricot verts are small, slender, dark green, young pod beans favored in France. Delicately flavored, they are more elegant then other green beans.

Hot-Pepper Sauce A splash of hot-pepper sauce adds zip to dishes. Countless varieties of hot-pepper sauce are made, with a rainbow of pepper colors and heat levels, so allow yourself the opportunity to experiment and find one you especially like.

Mangoes Juicy, sweet-fleshed fruit native to India and now cultivated in many tropical regions. When shopping for ripe mangoes, choose fruits that are aromatic at their stem ends.

Mirin A sweet Japanese cooking wine made by fermenting glutinous rice and sugar. The pale golden wine adds a rich flavor when added to a dish or dipping sauce.

Mustard, Dijon Originating in Dijon, France, this silky smooth and slightly tangy mustard contains brown or black mustard seeds, white wine, and herbs.

Oil The heat requirements and other ingredients of a recipe usually suggest which oil is appropriate to use. As a general rule, choose less-refined, more flavorful oils for uncooked uses, such as tossing raw or already cooked foods, and refined, blander oils for cooking.

Asian Sesame This amber-colored oil, pressed from toasted sesame seeds, has a rich, nutty flavor. Look for it in well-stocked markets and Asian groceries.

Canola This neutral-flavored oil, notable for its monounsaturated fats, is recommended for general cooking.

Grapeseed Pressed from grape seeds and mild in flavor, this all-purpose oil heats to high temperature without smoking, making it suitable for frying, and is also used in salad dressings and marinades.

Olive Made from the first pressing of the olives without the use of heat or chemicals, extra-virgin olive oil is clear green or brownish and has a fruity, slightly peppery flavor that is used to best advantage when it will not be cooked. Olive oils extracted using heat or chemicals, then filtered and blended to eliminate much of the olives' character, may be used for general cooking. In the past, such oil was labeled "pure olive oil." Today, it is simply labeled "olive oil."

Olives, Kalamata The most popular Greek variety, the Kalamata olive is almond shaped, purplish black, rich, and meaty. It is brine cured and then packed in oil or vinegar.

Herbs

Using fresh herbs is a great way to improve the flavor of your cooking. Dried herbs have their place, but fresh herbs usually bring brighter flavors to a dish.

Basil Used in kitchens throughout the Mediterranean and in Southeast Asia, fresh basil adds a highly aromatic, peppery flavor.

Chervil A delicate springtime herb with a taste reminiscent of parsley and anise. It goes particularly well with poultry and seafood.

Chives These slender, hollow, grass-like blades are used to give an onion-like flavor to dishes, without the bite.

Cilantro Also called fresh coriander or Chinese parsley, cilantro has a bright astringent taste. It is used extensively in Mexican, Asian, and Middle Eastern cuisines.

Lemongrass An from Southeast Asia, it resembles a green (spring) onion in shape but has a fresh lemony aroma and flavor. Use only the tender, creamy to pale yellow inner part from the bottom for cooking.

Marjoram A Mediterranean native, this herb has a milder, sweeter flavor than its cousin, oregano. It is best fresh. Pair it with tomatoes, eggplant, poultry and seafood.

Mint This refreshing herb is available in many varieties, with spearmint the most commonly found. Used fresh to flavor a broad range of savory preparations, including lamb, poultry, and vegetables.

Oregano Aromatic and spicy herb also known as wild marjoram. It is one of the few herbs that keeps its flavor when dried.

Parsley Also known as Italian parsley, this dark green Italian variety of the faintly peppery herb adds color and pleasing fresh flavor to dishes.

Rosemary This woody herb from the Mediterranean, with leaves like pine needles, has an assertive flavor. Always use in moderation. It is a particularly good complement to chicken and lamb.

Sage The soft, gray-green leaves of this Mediterranean herb are sweet and aromatic.

Savory A delicate herb which has a scent reminiscent of thyme and a faintly bitter, almost minty flavor. Add in small amounts to meat dishes or use to infuse vinegar.

Tarragon The slender, delicate, deep green leaves of tarragon impart an elegant, aniselike scent.

Onions This humble bulb vegetable, in the same family as leeks and garlic, is one of the most common and frequently used ingredients in the kitchen.

Green Also known as scallions or spring onions, green onions are the immature shoots of the bulb onion, with a narrow white base that has not yet begun to swell and long, flat green leaves, sometimes called "tops." They are mild in flavor.

Red These onions tend to be mild, slightly sweet, and purplish. They are delicious when used raw.

Yellow These are the familiar, all-purpose onions sold in supermarkets. Yellow onions are usually too harsh for serving raw, but they become rich and sweet when cooked.

Papaya A tropical fruit with a hollow center, which holds a shiny mass of small, slick black seeds, which are edible and have a slightly peppery flavor.

Pappadam Waffers A light crispy Indian wafer disc shaped made with chickpea and lentil flour spiced served with traditional Indian fare.

Paprika Red or orange-red, paprika is made from dried peppers. The finest paprikas come from Hungary and Spain in three basic types: sweet, medium-sweet, and hot. Sweet paprika, which is mild but still pungent, is the most versatile.

The best Spanish paprika, known as pimentón de La Vera, is made from smoked peppers, which give it a distinctive flavor.

Mushroom This popular edible fungus comes in numerous, increasingly available, flavorful varieties.

Cremini Closely related to common white mushrooms, cremini can be used whenever white mushrooms are called for, but they have a light brown color and firmer texture.

Morel Considered the king of all mushrooms, the morel has an intense, musky flavor that makes it highly sought after. The uncultivated mushroom has a dark, elongated, sponge-like cap and hollow stem. Morels are especially delicious in cream sauces and scrambled eggs.

Porcini Also known as cépe and bolete. Porcini (Italian for "little pigs") are indeed nicely plump, with a firm texture, sweet fragrance, and full, earthy flavor. An uncultivated variety, they have caps similar to cremini in shape and color, but their stems are thick and swollen.

Portobello Mature cremini mushrooms, portobellos have a rich smoky flavor and meat texture. Discard the thick, tough stems before cooking.

Shiitake The most popular mushroom in Japan and now widely cultivated. Fresh shiitake should have smooth, plump

caps, while better-quality dried ones have pale cracks in the caps surface. Dried shitake and chicnese black mushrooms are interchangeable. Shiitake take well to grilling, roasting, stir-frying, and sautéing.

White The cultivated, all-purpose mushroom sold in grocery stores. Sometimes called button mushrooms, although the term refers specifically to young, tender ones with closed caps. For general cooking try to find the medium sized mushrooms with little or no gills showing.

Ramps Also called wild leeks, ssertively garlic ramps grow wild in the U.S. If you cannot find them, substitute leeks or green onions.

Bell Pepper Also known as sweet peppers and capsicums, these flavorful, colorful peppers are delicious cooked on the grill, where they are charred and then peeled

Sake Sometimes referred to as "Japanese rice wine" it is made from grain, not fruit and has a relatively low alcohol count. It lends itself well to marinades and sauces.

Satay Popular in Southeast Asia, satay are strips of meat or poultry threaded onto skewers, grilled, and served with a spicy peanut-based dipping sauce.

Scallop A popular mullosk, plump and flavorful. The bivalves are shucked almost immediately after they are caught. The edible portion is actually the abductor muscle used to open and close the shell.

Shallots These small members of the onion family look like large cloves of garlic covered with papery bronze or reddish skin. Shallots have white flesh streaked with purple, a crisp texture, and a flavor more subtle than that of onions.

Shrimp Although often sold peeled and deveined, it's best to purchase shrimp (prawns) still in their shells if possible. Most shrimp have been previously frozen, and the shells help preserve their texture and flavor.

Spices An important part of any spice pantry, seeds, used whole or ground, add flavor, aroma, and texture to marinades, rubs, and other preparations.

Aniseed The seed of the anise plant, a member of the parsley family, aniseed has a licorice taste.

Coriander The dried ripe fruit of fresh coriander, or cilantro, these tiny, round, ridged seeds have an exotic flavor.

Cumin The seed of a member of the parsley family, cumin adds a sharp flavor to many Latin American and Indian dishes.

Five-spice Sometimes labeled "Chinese five-spice powder" this potent spice blend usually contains cloves, aniseeds or fennel seeds, star anise, cinnamon, Sichuan peppercorns, and sometimes ginger. It can used in both savory and sweet dishes.

Nutmeg The oval brown seed of a soft fruit, nutmeg has a warm, sweet, spicy flavor. It grows in a hard shell that is often in turn covered by the membrane that becomes mace.

Star anise A dried star-shaped seedpod of a Chinese evergreen tree. It is more bitter than aniseed and has a distinct licorice flavor.

Turmeric Like saffron, turmeric is valued both for its taste and its bright color. The root of a plant belonging to the ginger family, turmeric is used fresh and dried.

Tomatillos Although they look like small green tomatoes and are called *tomates verdes* in Mexico, tomatillos are not relatives ofthe tomato. They are for salsa verde, the popular Mexican table sauce.

Tomatoes The tomato comes in a wide range of sizes. The colors can vary from white to purple-black to reddish black to green striped zebra tomatoes which are somewhere in the middle.

Cherry Miniature, sweet tomatoes available in yellow, red, and orange. Look for red Sweet 100s or orange Sungolds, both especially sweet and intensely flavored.

Green Tomato Both a specific tomato variety and the unripe version of red tomatoes. The variety is eaten like any ripe tomato, while green tomatoes are often fried.

Roma Also known as plum or egg tomatoes, these have a meaty, flavorful flesh that is particularly good for making sauce

Tortilla Made from *Masa* a dough made by boiling dried corn kernels with skaed lime to remove their tough skins, and then grinding them to form a dough. Tortillas are use in traditional Mexican dishes such as quesadillas and often fried to make tortilla chips.

Vinegar Many types of vinegar are available, made from a variety of wines. They often add a nice amount of tartness to a dish.

Balsamic This aged vinegar is made from the unfermented grape juice of white Trebbiano grapes. Balsamic is aged for as long as 75 years

White Wine A pantry staple carried in most supermarkets, white wine vinegar is created by allowing white wine to ferment naturally over a period of months

Zest The colored portion of citrus peel, which is rich in flavorful oils. The white portion of the peel, called the pith, is bitter.

Index

First published in the USA by Time-Life Custom Publishing.

Originally published as Williams-Sonoma Lifestyle Series:
Casual Outdoor Dining (© 1998 Weldon Owen Inc.)
Chicken for Dinner (© 1998 Weldon Owen Inc.)
Classic Pasta at Home (© 1998 Weldon Owen Inc.)
Everyday Roasting (© 1998 Weldon Owen Inc.)
Fresh & Light (© 1998 Weldon Owen Inc.)
Holiday Celebrations (© 1998 Weldon Owen Inc.)
Soup for Supper (© 1998 Weldon Owen Inc.)
Vegetarian for All Seasons (© 1998 Weldon Owen Inc.)
Asian Flavors (© 1999 Weldon Owen Inc.)
Backyard Barbeque (© 1999 Weldon Owen Inc.)
Brunch Entertaining (© 1999 Weldon Owen Inc.)
Cooking From the Farmer's Market (© 1999 Weldon Owen Inc.)
Cooking for Yourself (© 1999 Weldon Owen Inc.)
Food & Wine Pairing (© 1999 Weldon Owen Inc.)
Holiday Cooking with Kids (© 1999 Weldon Owen Inc.)
Small Plates (© 1999 Weldon Owen Inc.)
Weekends with Friends (© 2000 Weldon Owen Inc.)

In collaboration with Williams-Sonoma Inc.
3250 Van Ness Avenue, San Francisco, CA 94109

Oxmoor House.

OXMOOR HOUSE INC.
Oxmoor House books are distributed by Sunset Books
80 Willow Road, Menlo Park, CA 94025
Telephone: 650-321-3600 Fax 650-324-1532
Vice President/General Manager: Rich Smeby
National Accounts Manager/Special Sales: Brad Moses

Oxmoor House and Sunset Books are divisions of
Southern Progress Corporation

WILLIAMS-SONOMA
Founder and Vice-Chairman: Chuck Williams

WELDON OWEN INC.
Chief Executive Officer: John Owen
President and Chief Operating Officer: Terry Newell
President and Chief Operating Officer: Christine E. Munson
Vice President International Sales: Stuart Laurence

Creative Director: Gaye Allen
Publisher: Hannah Rahill
Senior Designer: Kara Church
Senior Editor: Jennifer Newens
Associate Editor: Lauren Hancock
Production Director: Chris Hemesath
Production and Reprint Coordinator: Todd Rechner
Color Manager: Teri Bell

Williams-Sonoma Grilling & Roasting was conceived and
produced by Weldon Owen Inc.
814 Montgomery Street, San Francisco, CA 94133
Copyright © 2007 Weldon Owen Inc.
and Williams-Sonoma Inc.

First printed in 2007.
10 9 8 7 6 5 4 3 2 1

ISBN-10: 0-8487-3167-0
ISBN-13: 978-0-8487-3167-0

Printed in China by SNP Leefung Printers Ltd.

CREDITS
Authors: Georgeanne Brennan: Pages 25, 33, 47–48, 115, 129, 138, 147, 150, 165, 179, 186, 200, 203, 235, 253, 262, 265, 273; Heidi Haughty Cusick; Pages 44, 59, 68–73, 98, 228, 278; Lane Crowther: Pages 50, 65, 148, 156, 257; Janet Fletcher: Pages 19, 34, 55, 60, 116, 185; Joyce Goldstein: Pages 81, 121, 152, 169–178, 208–211, 219, 258; Pamela Sheldon Johns: Pages 37, 232; Joyce Jue: Pages 22, 26–28, 77–78, 82, 97, 207, 212, 281; Susan Manlin Katzman: Pages 66; Betty Rosbottom: Pages 62, 126, 141, 195, 199, 203; Janeen Sarlin: Pages 18, 51–52, 56, 61, 74, 107, 119, 122–125, 130–134, 155, 163, 166, 182, 192, 204, 224, 234, 238, 241, 245–249, 254, 266, 270, 274; Phillip Stephen Schultz: Pages 29, 85–91, 101, 108–112, 118, 137, 144, 160, 164, 188–191, 196, 215–216, 220, 227, 231, 242, 252, 269, 277, 282,–286; Marie Simmons: Pages 14, 30, 181, 261; Joanne Weir: Pages 17, 21, 38–41, 250

Photographers: Jeff Tucker and Kevin Hossler (cover); Richard Eskite (Introduction and recipe photography); Joyce Ouderk Pool (photography for pages 63, 67, 127, 141, 159, 194, 203).

ACKNOWLEDGMENTS
Weldon Owen would like to thank Kevin Crafts, Lesli Neilson, and Kate Washington for all their expertise, assistance, and hard work.

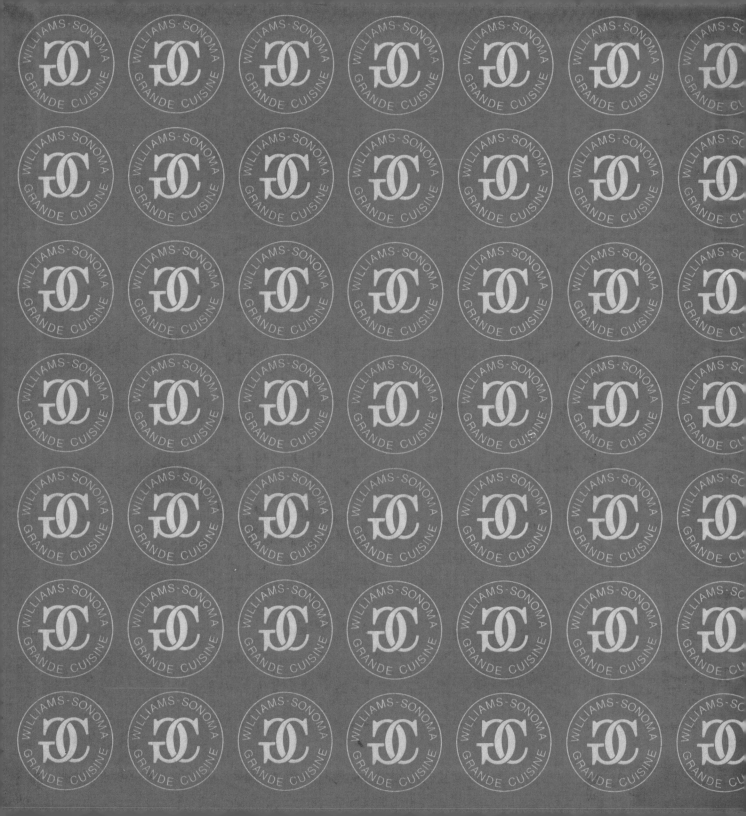